Bi
Reimagining Between the Lines

Edited by
Megan Rohrer & Daniel Tisdel

FEATURING WRITING BY:

RICHARD CLEAVER ‡ CHARLES FEATHERSTONE
MALCOLM HIMSCHOOT ‡ THOM LONGINO
KATHRYN MUYSKENS ‡ EMILY OLSEN
LAUREL KAPROS ROHRER ‡ MEGAN ROHRER
DANIEL TISDEL ‡ AMANDA ZENTZ-ALO

© 2014 Wilgefortis

BIBLE STORIES
Reimagining Between the Lines
Edited by Megan Rohrer and Daniel Tisdel

Cover Design by Megan Rohrer
Photos of street art in Brazil by Megan Rohrer

All rights reserved under International and Pan-American Copyright Conventions. Published in the United States by Wilgefortis.

Except for brief quotations in critical articles or reviews, no part of this book may be reproduced in any form without the permission of the author.

First Printing

ISBN: 978-1-312-37937-4

THANK YOU

Megan would like to thank the members and friends of Grace Evangelical Lutheran Church in San Francisco who support me and literally pay my rent. Special thanks to Laurel, my wife. Her love and support means the world to me. Additionally, her love of cleaning allows me to write instead of doing chores. Last but not least, a big fist bump to the God of all, who helps me transform the stuff of my dreams into tangible books, gardens and prescription glasses for the homeless.

Dan would like to thank God who keeps amazing him despite his penchant for getting in the way. He thanks his family and friends for supporting him, especially his Mom and Stepdad, Brother, awesome niece Maia, and his girlfriend Emily (also a contributor in this book) all of whom patiently listen to his many ideas and rants. He wants to thank Megan for involving him in this book and the congregations and leadership of First Evangelical Lutheran Church, Gypsum; Good Shepherd Lutheran, Glenwood Springs; and Our Saviors Lutheran Church, Denver; all of whom support him in myriad and wonderful ways.

GIVING BACK

The proceeds of this book will support Welcome - a communal response to poverty. Welcome seeks to provide a faithful response to poverty and to improve the quality of life for individuals in our community by providing: hospitality; education; food; and referrals for housing, health care and drug and alcohol treatment. You can learn more about Welcome at the end of this book or by visiting: www.sfwelcome.org.

Introduction — 5
- BIRTHING BIBLE STORIES // MEGAN ROHRER — 6
- INSPIRED BY FICTION // DANIEL TISDEL — 7

In the Beginning — 10
- GENESIS // MEGAN ROHRER — 10
- BROTHERS // CHARLES FEATHERSTONE — 15
- THE UNDEAD // CHARLES FEATHERSTONE — 38
- LACED // MALCOLM HIMSCHOOT — 45
- MY NAME IS JOB // KATHRYN MUYSKENS — 51

The Gospel According to Us — 57
- TOMATO SEEDS // EMILY OLSEN — 57
- THE JACKASS GOSPEL // AMANDA ZENTZ-ALO — 68
- LEFT BEHIND… IN A BOAT // DANIEL TISDEL — 71
- TO BLEED // LAUREL KAPROS ROHRER — 74
- LEGION // DANIEL TISDEL — 78
- THE PARABLE OF LAZARUS AND THE RICH MAN // THOM LONGINO — 83

Acts and Letters — 85
- THE TESTIMONY OF BACHOS // RICHARD CLEAVER — 85
- A STREET CALLED STRAIGHT // CHARLES FEATHERSTONE — 109
- 3 CORINTHIANS // MEGAN ROHRER — 117

Revelations — 119
- DREAMS OF DREAMS OF DREAMS // MEGAN ROHRER — 119

About the Authors — 123

Introduction

Birthing Bible Stories   //   Megan Rohrer

Each week, for as long as I can remember, I have heard about someone who was hurt when a bible story was twisted into a weapon. When someone has done this to me, no amount of context, historical review or conversation about the wild ways of the Holy Spirit has ever changed the mind of the bible thumper.

Bible Stories: Reimagining Between the Lines is a fictional collection inspired by the aches and pains of our contemporary world. Using well known and hidden stories of the Bible, some authors reset the time or place of the story. Others added additional materials that reflect upon contemporary issues, read between the lines of the original story, wrote a better storyline for forgotten characters or included historical insight rewritten in a way that provides a richer understanding of the original story.

I hope this book will inspire you to reconnect with the Bible. If you find that there are parts of the original or this book that don't work for you, I give you permission to stick with the stories that inspire you to love yourself, your family and your neighbors. The stories that make you mad that injustice exists (in the text or in the world) are meant to provoke you to either get off your butt and do something, or write a check to those who make the world a little better for all of us.

Whether you read every page or you simply use this book to fill your bookshelf, I hope it inspires you to reimagine your world and remember that, no matter what anyone says, God loves you and always with you.

Pastor Megan Rohrer
December 2014
San Francisco

P.S. You're welcome to join me any Sunday, in person or online, at Grace Lutheran in San Francisco. You can learn more at www.gracesf.com

Inspired by Fiction   //   Daniel Tisdel

I admit that I didn't grow up loving the Bible. The way I was raised, I was given a lot of freedom in how I thought and how I acted. I chose, on my own, to go to church because I saw the value of organized religion for me personally, and for society. I know that I have heard that term, "Organized Religion," used as a code word for all that is wrong with churches, but for me, church has always been a place where I felt safe and loved, a place which made a difference in people's lives, and a place where I was free to believe the way I thought best. I know I am lucky that this was my experience with "Organized Religion". In the church I grew up in, I was allowed to think freely, I was allowed to believe or not believe the way I wanted. I was allowed to grow and think within the realm of my faith and I think that freedom is part of why I grew to love the Bible.

As I grew in my faith, I was able to start asking questions about scripture; questions which often did not have answers. I could imagine the untold stories. I started to see characters that appeared far too briefly in the scripture and wondered about the rest of their story. I read sections of scripture and wondered what happened next or what else was going on. The scriptures were made even more alive for me because I was free to imagine the scene, free to imagine what was unrecorded or even unsaid. The scripture began to jump off the page for me. To be fair, they always had life and truth and were never less than holy and important, but being able to creatively read and listen made them more *interesting*.

One day I was sitting with a friend, needing something to do to pass the time. I was encouraged to read the Bible, which was not foreign to me but still not something I did very often for fun. I opened the Bible to the story of the Gerasene Demoniac, the man possessed by demons; demons which Jesus released into a herd of pigs. After reading it, I started to ask many questions. What happened next? Did the man stay there or was he sent away? Did he return to a normal life? How did he get that way? How long had he been possessed? What was his name? (It was never said in scripture). My friend encouraged me to write about it, to make up a purely fictional story with this scripture as a starting point. I did and it was an interesting and worthwhile exercise. Not so much because the story was any good, but because it opened my eyes to the untold stories of the Bible. For your interest, I have included that original story in this volume.

That first story was one of many events in my life that helped guide me to go to seminary and become a pastor. I became intensely curious about scripture. I wondered why we heard many stories quite often and rarely heard other stories. I re-discovered the richness of scripture.

Then I found myself sitting next to Pastor Megan Rohrer attending "Open Cathedral" in the Mission district of San Francisco. The scripture of Jesus calling the brothers James and John was read where the brothers dropped the nets they were mending with their father Zebedee and followed a complete stranger, Jesus, as he invited them from the beach. I turned to Megan and wondered aloud how Zebedee must have felt at that moment. Megan replied that she wondered the same thing and right there, sitting on a cold concrete wall in the middle of a public worship service, we threw out names and stories that we had always wondered about. We later came up with a list of forty or fifty Biblical names or stories that we wanted more information about.

Pastor Megan also opened up an idea I hadn't considered before. What would these stories that we knew so well feel like if they were recast in a different time or different setting? What if the stories of the Bible happened in the present day? How would they look the same? In which ways would they be necessarily different? None of this is to take anything away from the original scripture or to attempt some sort of strange translation but instead to open the scriptures up, as they had been opened for us, in a new and amazing way.

The possibilities were endless, and though Pastor Megan had published several times, the idea of turning this into a book seemed daunting. It turns out that our experience of reimagining these texts was not a wholly original idea. Many ideas were brewing in the minds of people we knew and when we invited them, people were more than willing to contribute. The results have been amazing so far, and reading the submissions of so many creative people helped me to realize how inspirational scripture can be, how it can be comfortably hand in hand with creative thinking and open minds. I hope you enjoy reading these stories as much as I have.

Daniel Tisdel
Gypsum, Colorado
December 2014

In the Beginning

Genesis // Megan Rohrer

Overwhelmed by love, I was caught in a euphoric fog. I had full lungs, a full heart and everything was wonderful and new. Then one day along came a snake. Fear and shame suddenly surrounded me as I heard a voice from the green reptile that was slithering around my ankle: "It can all go as quickly as it came you know. Change is inevitable and you, my dear, will be stretched and scarred before you settle into something as sweet as love. You had to learn to walk, you will have to learn to love and starting now, you need to learn to breathe."

The snake was gone before I could respond, but the words continued to ricochet in my ears. When the swell of breath first entered my lungs it was automatic, I did it without thinking. God and love were so natural to me, I had no idea that I would later wish that I was taking notes. And soon that automatic bodily breath that sent oxygen to my brain was engulfed and stymied by fear and shame. I began to feel the tightness in my lungs of asthma.

While I was in the hazy fog of new love, the world had built itself up around me. A swirling infrastructure of concrete pulsed across the land congested and clogged with the things that people thought would help them to breathe more fully. And as the world got more crowded some people built concrete walls to ensure that they could own a bit of air where only they could breathe. Some built their houses so high, they thought they could reach into the sky and pull God down from God's thrown. God got one of those motorized solar powered chairs to dash through the heavens with a flaming exhaust that kept people on their toes.

But people chose not to chase after God. Instead a business man started telling people that they could spend time with God after they breathed no more, and that they should spend their time on earth enjoying themselves. That sounded a bit more fun than grasping at a moving God who was only remembered as a voice trailing from a lingering flame. So, the people turned to the marketing men to find out what to do. That business man knew that if he could keep people focused like a magician on enough shiny things, the right gadgets and the latest fall fashions that they would forget that they had lost their breath. And they did forget, or perhaps they didn't know that lungs can only be filled with air and that hearts are made to love and to circulate oxygenated blood throughout a sensuous body. Wise advertisers made sure that the newest car and twinkling gizmos, that breathless people could not afford, would always distract them from the hollowness that lingered.

Suddenly my ears and eyes were open. I saw stacks of rubble and loads of junk that piled toward the sky. There were stacks of plastic and hair goo, not to mention piles of anti-aging gunk. There were miles of half-finished hobbies and crafts that were discarded and forgotten when the newest distraction came along. There were even discarded people, thrown away and forgotten. Some lay about openly on cardboard, because they were so universally regarded as waste that they were nearly indistinguishable from the assorted bits of last year's miracle devices and half eaten dishes that are now proven to cause cancer or an undesired swelling in teenage ankles that they scavenged through.

Some people were discarded more subtly with glances or by seemingly nice people who just pretended to listen. Some were deemed less profitable and were given pink slips as they became the bottom line. And still, others were told they needed to do everything to buy drugs they couldn't afford in order to survive long enough to learn that it was really the drugs that were killing them.

The trash on the ground wasn't the end of it; they had also trashed the air. All their lives they had been told that if the car companies weren't doing well, that they would lose their jobs, then their homes, then their loves and finally their lives. So they bought cars believing that if they had them in constant motion they wouldn't have to face the fact that they were not in control of the chaos that swirled all around them. Yes, nothing leads you to believe that you are in control of your life more than driving a car. As long as you've got gas and a good mechanic you can make it through anything, right?

They forgot that they needed God. They forgot they needed love and breath. And the more they forgot the more they drove. The more they drove the more they trashed the air and the less they could breathe. So, what else could they do? They just keep driving. How did my marshy riverbed become a concrete highway? Caught up in my fear and shame I didn't notice that you had moved so far away too. I was in a swirling San Francisco metropolis and you were somewhere in rural Iowa, where you said the air was fresher and it was easier to breathe. I was still drifting in and out of my fog and you were changing with the seasons.

I've heard this story before, the glaciers began to move through the Midwest, melted and there was a huge flood. Noah built that boat and all the animals lined up in twos, or more, depending on the version you read. Such a great love story all those pairs of animals getting on the big boat venturing into the new world. And yet, they never talk about the line getting off the boat. Was it a loving exit or was it like getting off the Titanic? Anyway, it's the end of the story that's important. And in love it seems that it is always the end of the story that tailors how we tell the beginning. And in the end God declares that never again will God try to kill everyone to remake the world.

And yet, here we are as the air gets thicker and darker and the world gets hot. They say the glaciers have already begun melting and I wonder who is going to have the guts to build the big boat. But, I imagine that there will be no boat, just a bunch of faces pointed to the heavens raising angry fists and shouting: "You said you would never do this again." And then the booming voice will say, "I didn't do it this time. You wanted to believe that you were right and in control so badly. But sadly, the only way to do that was to get rid of everyone else. I'd die to make it better, but I don't know if even that would help at this point."

All we had to do was breathe. The earth longed to show us how love brought everything into bloom and perhaps if we were really looking we would see it. But like babies with a shiny set of keys, we were distracted. And with our hands firmly on the etch-e-sketch we shake and shake and begin again. What will we create this time? Will we remember that it is so much easier to tear it all down then to build it up again?

Thankfully this end is a beginning, and this story will begin again and again before it ends.

Brothers // Charles Featherstone

Isaac loved to watch the sun set.

There was something about seeing the colors of the sun and the sky change, especially when the sky was clear – as it was so often in the summer time. It was a thing to behold, Isaac thought. A truly wondrous thing to behold.

Today was no exception. It had been a long, hot day, and now it was almost over. Isaac sat on the side of a little hill, watching the cloudless sky grow pink and orange, gazing over the small collection of goats and sheep slowly chewing their way across the scrub. It was the dry season, he thought, it hadn't rained in some months. And it wouldn't rain again for another few months.

God willing.

Which meant that Isaac would soon have to pack everyone up and move. His wife, his slaves, his animals, all to the next well, to better pasture. This place, with its spring and its trees, was the closest thing Isaac and his family had to a real home. But they frequently had to leave, to follow the rains, to follow pasture. They were nomads, Isaac and his family, and the most they could claim about this land is that their ancestors were buried here.

Ancestors. The only permanent structure Isaac's family had ever built was for the dead, slowly and painfully hewn out of rock. Isaac's mother, rest in that cave.

Tomorrow, she would no longer be alone.

Rain or shine, frigid cold or searing heat, sandstorm and drought, Isaac's family lived in a collection of tents, flimsy homes of cloth and animal skin, parts of which were first made long before Isaac was born. In some places, such as here, the tents would stay up for months. No house of wood or brick for them. There was no point, not when they had to move so much, to find a place to water their stock.

Isaac looked down at his side and the saw the long stick

his father had carved and polished the stick he used to prod and poke reluctant sheep. He picked it up and held it tight in his curved hands. It was smooth, worn, shiny. It was an old thing, like some of the tent poles, made smooth by years of handling. He watched his father carve this stick, fashioning it from a long, straight tree branch that had fallen from the terebinths nearby. He'd watched his father use that stick, keeping the sheep and the goats in line as he moved them along. But it was a long, heavy stick, and it had other unpleasant uses, such as on the occasional and unfortunate insubordinate slave who failed to heed his father's commands quickly enough.

His father even raised it a time or two at Isaac, his face twisted with rage, spittle spewing from his mouth as he breathed fire and threats. At times like this, Isaac thought his father seemed completely undone by his anger. Until his father saw the terror in his son's eyes, and remembered. And his father would drop the stick, a look of shame eclipsing his entire face. He would look away — his father rarely looked directly at Isaac, rarely made eye contact, not after that day. He would walk away. Off into the bright heat of the day, or the rain, or the dark, or once even into a sandstorm. And not come back, not for a long while.

"This is my stick now," Isaac said softly to himself as he twirled the stick in the air. He stuck the end in the ground, looking to all the world like a miniature version of the poles some of the neighbors worshiped. He squinted, looking at the sun, at the bands of red and orange and pink and purple that painted the dome of the sky. At the sheep as they grazed.

"These are my sheep now," he said, looking at the herd grazing quietly. He started to count them, as he had so many times before, but stopped.

"All of this is mine now. All of it," he whispered softly, exhaling the words. There was no celebration in this, no sorrow. It just was.

"Good God, what will I do with it all?"

* * *

It had seemed to his son that Abraham would never die. Could never die. He was a big man, larger than life, tall and loud and overwhelming. His voice seemed to him like it could call to the horizons, even command rain and fire from the sky. He stood over everyone, apart from everyone, an intense and purposeful look in his eyes. Abraham was a force to be reckoned with, and Isaac knew that from a very young age. It seemed to Isaac that Abraham did what he wanted, lived as he pleased, went where he chose. You simply went along with him or got out his way.

Because of this, it was hard for Isaac to make sense of the things Abraham said of LORD, who seemed to be a constant presence in Abraham's life. His father, so strong, so self-possessed, so willful, spoke of LORD as this person who commanded him, compelled him, forced him, told him. It made no sense to Isaac. Who could command his father? Especially to do some of the strange and awful things his father had done.

And why, Isaac wondered, hadn't LORD ever spoken to him? If Abraham was so beloved, and Isaac was this child of promise – Abraham never stopped reminding him of that, never ceased calling him "my son of promise," even long after they stopped exchanging civil words to each other – then why had LORD been so silent? Why had he not talked to Isaac the way he had talked to Abraham?

They had been words Isaac had screamed at his father once, long after the horrible day. Long after his mother Sarah died of a broken heart.

"Your LORD, he speaks to you! He loves you! He visits you! Why doesn't your LORD speak to me? Why don't I get so much as a whisper? Why does he leave me so alone? Or does he hate me as much as you do!?"

It always seemed to hurt Abraham deeply and visibly whenever Isaac accused Abraham of hating him. Neither could understand the other, and neither seemed willing to try. But that day, after those words, Abraham looked at his son. His rage evaporated, and he crumpled. His eyes glistened with tears, and for a brief moment, he looked right at his son. Right into his angry boy's soul.

17

"My dear child of laughter, you do not want LORD to speak to you. He commands terrible, awful, inexplicable things. None of what he says or does makes sense." His voice stopped, and he seemed overwhelmed by regret, or maybe sorrow. "I would not wish his friendship upon you for anything in the world. Be grateful he does not speak to you. That he has nothing to do with you. Be grateful."

Isaac hated that answer. For a long time, he passionately hated his father.

And he hated LORD too.

Yet, it was hard for Isaac to watch his father get old, to become bent over, to loose strength and stamina, to have his senses and reason slowly slip away from him. To wheeze and wince with pain in his joints and not be able to keep up even with the goats. One day, not long ago, Abraham could no longer rise up out of bed. And then he breathed his last. He was gone.

That was yesterday. The body of the man whose life had been so large now lay, cold and gray, in a tent. He would be buried tomorrow, soon after sunrise. Regardless.

A breeze was beginning to blow from the west. It wasn't cool, not like evening breezes from right off the sea. It was not the right time of year for cool breezes. But it felt good all the same.

He heard footsteps in the gravel behind him. Isaac turned around and looked up. It was Rebekah, his wife. She looked tired, and she held tightly to her headscarf as it wanted to catch the wind and fly away.

"Dinner is ready. There's bread, lamb, figs, dates, and wine. The servants are afraid things will get cold." She paused. "So, do you know if he's even coming?"

Isaac stood up, brushed the dirt and leaves off his robe. "I love you, Little Lamb." He put his arm around her and held her loosely. She struggled slightly, more out of propriety than anything else. "People are watching!" she would often tell Isaac if he got too affectionate in public. He let go and smiled at her. She blushed.

He always thought her smile meant she was playing when

she did this, when she gently pushed him away or chided him for trying to kiss her. But no, Rebekah really wasn't comfortable with public displays of affection, not even around the slaves. She loved Isaac deeply, loved touching him and being touched, holding him and being held. She simply did not like being the center of that kind of public attention.

But lately, he loved to touch her belly, which had grown round with the child she'd been carrying for maybe six months now. He couldn't look at her without being overwhelmed by the sight of it all, he couldn't introduce her to strangers and visitors without feeling an incredible sense of pride. "Look what I did!" he wanted to tell the world.

She smiled, and held his hand.

"I swear upon God Most High, it feels like there are two children in there, already fighting each other."

He smiled and laughed slightly.

"We aren't that lucky, Little Lamb," he replied. "Remember the struggle my father had to go through just to have me? That sort of thing doesn't happen to us. I consider us lucky that we're having a child without divine intervention."

She blushed again and laughed and looked down at the ground. A scurrying lizard caught her eye, and she followed it just long enough to lose her train of thought. Something about dinner.

"How long has it been since you've seen him?"

Isaac thought. "I really don't remember. A long time. He was keeping sheep somewhere far south of here, but that was some years ago. I don't know what he does now."

The two stood holding each other, the breeze wrapping their bodies.

"Look, if my brother comes, he comes. I was told last week he and some of his people should be close. So, I sent some messengers out to try and find them. They probably won't find him, and that's okay."

Isaac inhaled. And then breathed out.

"We bury the old man tomorrow regardless. Let's wait a little while longer, but tell the servants they can eat now." She nodded and turned to walk away. "Make sure there is plenty of wine left. I'm not going to welcome my half-brother without wine!"

No, he knew exactly what he'd do with it all. He'd love his wife, and raise his family. Whatever LORD had told Abraham, whatever promises LORD had made over the years, none of it mattered much to Isaac. Not as silent as LORD had been.

* * *

Isaac first saw the forms come slowly over the hill. Three lumps, moving slowly, along the dirt road that cut through the valley. The sun had almost vanished below the horizon, and he started playing a little game with himself – would the forms get to him before the sky got too dark to see much? Or not? As they ambled along the road, Isaac noticed the sky slowly turning from pink to purple, deeper and darker shades of blue slowly creeping up from the dome's eastern edge.

The breeze was dying down, and the air was cool enough now to be called comfortable.

Isaac found it was becoming difficult to make out much about the forms coming his way. There was still some light left, and he could tell the animals were camels – three of them, with two riders dressed in flowing white robes and white turbans. The third camel was packed to bulging, the mass or cargo swaying and shifting slightly with every step.

He stood up. Would he recognize his brother after this long? Would his brother recognize him?

"Peace and blessings be with you!" He shouted when the two travelers and their three camels came within hearing distance.

The front rider raised his right hand in greeting. He was close enough now, Isaac could make out details. He was clearly older and bigger than the other camel rider. He had a beard, and a somewhat weathered face. His eyes were large, and brown, and even in the dim light they sparkled. With a sense of mischief or wonder Isaac could not be sure.

"And also with you!" the front rider responded. He pulled on the camel's reins and the animal came to a stop. After it had finished kneeling, the front rider quickly dismounted and adjusted his turban. He shook each of his legs, stretching them out after the long ride.

"It never gets any easier," he said, pacing a bit. He looked at Isaac.

"Ishmael? Is it really you?"

He smiled. With the sun long set, and the sky quickly covering itself in darkness, his eyes seemed to flash with their own light.

"Who else is going to help you help you wrap that old man up in a shroud and lay to him to rest in a cave?"

They grasped hands, and then embraced. They kissed each other on the cheek and then hugged each other tight. Then they stood back.

"Let me look at you, little brother. It has been a long time. Longer than I can count!"

Isaac, unsure what to feel, was suddenly overcome by a wave of awkwardness. How long had it been? He couldn't really remember. They had only really known each other as names, mostly, and as family stories, seeing each other occasionally when Abraham and his family made their usual summer and fall circuit of grazing lands, as both families wandered with their livestock. While Isaac knew Ishmael was his brother – his "half-brother by that miserable woman" as his mother always called him – he felt more like a distant cousin. Ishmael was a whole decade older than Isaac, and by the time Isaac was old enough to play, Ishmael was busy working – hunting, tending the sheep, helping the men in what had become his mother's tribe.

And then, one summer, they were gone. Isaac never knew where they'd gone, and if Abraham had learned, he never told his son.

"It's good to see you. However long it has been, much has happened! I've done pretty well for myself, and I have brought some things for you and your family!"

Isaac hadn't expected Ishmael to be so ... friendly. He'd been dreading this meeting because he wasn't sure what Ishmael would think of him. Sometimes, when Isaac thought about his father, it was impossible for him to dismiss the anger and self-pity that came with many of those memories, at least until he thought of his brother Ishmael. In many ways, Isaac thought, Ishmael had it worse.

"That's kind of you," Isaac responded. "Oh, I've forgotten my manners! Please, come, partake of our hospitality. Wash your feet! We have roast lamb – I remember how much you like roast lamb – bread, wine, figs and even some cucumbers!"

Ishmael nodded.

"And I have forgotten mine. This is my oldest son, Nebaioth. He is my indispensable right hand; I would not be anywhere near as successful without him." He motioned to his son, who then bid his camel to kneel. The young man, a tall and lanky lad dismounted and joined his father.

"You can hobble your camels here in this field. I have people looking after my sheep, and they can take them to graze some trees tomorrow morning."

"Excellent!" Ishmael exclaimed. The boy was silent, intensely looking at his father, observing everything, saying nothing.

"And everything on that third camel is yours. We have frankincense, dates from Arabia, and a few delicacies you have probably never seen before." He turned and held out his hand, sweeping over the camel standing in the distance as if he were trying to sell an entire heard of goats. "You can't keep the camel, though. I still need that."

Isaac laughed slightly, the two hugged again, and Isaac turned to Nebaioth.

"It is good to meet you, nephew."

"Peace be with you, uncle," the boy said. "My father has told me a lot about you."

"Oh, has he?"

"All bad, I promise," Ishmael broke in. He laughed. The boy finally smiled.

"No, not all bad, father." Nebaioth was slightly embarrassed.

Ishmael whistled. The two kneeling camels rose, and he motioned his son to take their reins. He grabbed the reins of the pack camel, and together with Isaac, began walking toward the cluster of tents that marked Isaac's home.

"You wouldn't happen to have a daughter old enough for Nebaioth to marry? The boy will be old enough soon, and it is high time he married. It would be good to marry a cousin, if he could. To keep things in the family. He's a serious boy, but as I said, without his seriousness, I wouldn't be so successful."

Isaac smiled and shook his head.

"No, sorry. I only got married a few years ago, and we are only expecting our first child. Rebekah – a distant cousin from Aram, my father sent his slave Eleazar all the way back home just to make sure I didn't marry a local girl – swears she's carrying two, but I keep telling her, remember who you married."

"Well, perhaps later. There will be time." He was silent for a moment. "Say, we don't have any other brothers or sisters do we?"

Isaac looked at Ishmael.

"After my mother died, father remarried. More than once. I lost track of how many wives and concubines he took. It seemed like a new woman every new moon for a time. And he had a whole mess of children. Funny, but once the pressure was off, once LORD was no longer breathing down his neck and making promises, God but that man could beget children."

Ishmael looked around. He cocked his ear, like he was listening for something. He heard crickets, the breeze, the occasional bleat of sheep in the distance. The expression on his face showed he clearly wasn't finding it.

"I'd expect the sounds of children running around. It's just after sunset during the hottest time of year, what better time to chase and play games. Where are they?"

Isaac swallowed.

"He sent them away. All of them. Before he died. They live somewhere that way, far away," he pointed in the direction of the hills where the sun rose. "I have no idea where. He provided well for them, but he wanted to make sure this, all of this, was mine. So, he sent them away."

Ishmael stopped and sighed. There was a slightly pained look on his face, an old but familiar feeling, a wound inflicted long ago that had since scarred thickly over. He looked in the direction of Isaac's outstretched hand. There was only darkness, an unknown wilderness, and the vague outline of hills as the stars began winking to life.

"He was good at that," he said.

* * *

Ishmael leaned back on his cushion, trying not to spill anything from his bowl of wine. It was good, the wine, sweet, and strong. He talked and he drank, he drank and he talked, and Isaac wasn't entirely sure how it was he could drink so much wine and talk so much at the same time. It didn't bother him much, though, as Ishmael was a good storyteller. He was fun to listen to. His eyes flashed constantly in the firelight, and his hands moved wildly to illustrate each point in his story. It seemed to Isaac that if you cut off Ishmael's hands, he would suddenly be unable to speak.

"... and so, one year we moved the flocks to another field, farther east then we'd ever been. It was the first year of the drought, remember that? A camel caravan coming from the south stopped at an oasis where we were watering our sheep. That's where I met Qureysh. I'd just gotten married, and was out watering the sheep when the camels arrived. Well, I offered to water Qureysh's camels for him. He was impressed with the job I did, said I showed 'initiative,' and so he talked to the head of my mother's tribe – she'd married again, to a group of desert dwellers in the wilderness of Sinai – and, thinking I was a slave, asked him how much he could buy me for?"

Ishmael laughed.

"The head of the tribe and I really ought to remember his name, since he did marry my mother, but you know, I don't, told Qureysh I wasn't *anyone's* slave. He was good like that. So, Qureysh wanted to know if I wanted to come with him, to Damascus, and learn how to be a merchant? I mean, assuming it was okay with the head of the tribe. And he let me go. So, I joined Qureysh. I've done pretty well, married one of his daughters, and have a nice little house in an oasis community many days south of here."

"How many wives do you have?"

"I have..." Ishmael paused and pretended to count on his fingers. "I have three. Lovely women, all of them, and they get along wonderfully. They live as befits the wives of a wealthy and prosperous merchant. I think it helps that I'm gone half the year. Mostly on the long path to Damascus, but sometimes I go as far south as Sheba, mostly to show my face, so that the people my agents and hired men trade with never forget who they are really doing business with."

He took a big gulp of wine again.

"Still, I miss this, little brother, this beautiful and wonderful simplicity. Living in a tent. Tending sheep. Moving to follow the pasture. It's a good life. A simple life. I do miss it. Nothing about being a merchant is simple. I think that's why I spend as much time with the caravans as I do, because I miss the wandering. A lot of other wealthy merchants aren't nearly as hands-on as I am. But I want my sons to know what it means to work."

Isaac sat his wine down on the small table in front of them. He sat up, and adjusted the cushion behind his back.

"You miss this? Really?"

It was silent as the two men looked at each other, the only sound was the popping of the fire between them and the occasional snapping of sheep bones in the jaws the Isaac's dogs outside the tent.

"I do," Ishmael said. He was quiet for a minute, looking down in his bowl of wine.

"I envied you. For years. You had our father. He would visit occasionally, but you really had him. All to yourself." Ishmael took a breath. "You know, I never liked your mother. In fact, for a long time, I hated her. It was her fault. All her fault. I'm her fault. She pushes my mother Hagar on Abraham, thinking something needed to be done to make the promise of LORD come true. And then, once I'm around, once Abraham has an actual son, she gets angry, jealous, and once you come, she tosses us out first chance she got."

He took another long drink of wine.

"That son of a slave woman," he continued, his voice assuming higher pitch, imitating Isaac's mother, "He will not live in my house! He will inherit nothing!"

"And he listened to her. This man, who stood up to LORD when LORD was going to flatten Sodom, and bargained for the lives of people he didn't even know, tossed his own son out!"

Ishmael's eyes flashed, shining bright with a fire of their own. He looked intensely at Isaac.

"You had him! All to yourself! He was there, to teach you, show you, be with you! He was your father! But not for me! He was just some stud of the field who impregnated my mother, and then sent her away, to die of thirst in the wilderness!"

Ishmael drank deeply from his wine bowl. He swallowed hard.

"Oh, how he ached for you! You, you were the long-hoped for child of promise! Me? I, I was just an afterthought. I was just..." Ishmael paused and looked down into his wine bowl.

"I was just an accident."

Isaac avoided Ishmael's gaze. He could feel the anger and sorrow in his brother's voice. He breathed out, held the emptiness in his lungs for a moment, and then inhaled.

"At least he never tried to kill you."

Ishmael's look went from anger to shock. His eyes grew wide.

"What?"

"You mean no one ever told you?"

"No."

Isaac took another deep drink of wine. His bowl was almost empty. He looked away from Ishmael, toward Nebaioth, who looked on as the two men spoke. Nebaioth's eyes met Isaac's, and the two looked at each for what felt to Isaac like an eternal moment.

"No, of course not. Why would they? One day, when I was a little younger than Nebaioth is now, LORD spoke to Abraham. 'Take your son, your only son Isaac' -- LORD never seemed to remember you -- 'and take him far away and offer him there as a burnt offering.' I didn't hear these words, of course, he told me all this later. Father just told me to pack the animals, that we are going someplace. Someplace far away.

"So I do this. And on the third day, we stop. We've got a donkey loaded with wood we cut the previous day, and he tells me, 'This is the place.' So he sets everything up, arranges the wood and lights the fire and gets out the sacrificial knife, and I'm looking around. There's no sheep there. No goat. Nothing.

"So I ask him, 'Father, we've got the wood and the fire, but where is the lamb?' He mumbles something about LORD providing, and then he takes out two long strips of leather..."

Isaac shudders. His eyes begin to tear up. He stops, takes a breath.

"I'm sorry, I haven't told this story in a long time. Where was I? Right, leather straps. He comes to me and starts binding my wrists and my ankles. That's when I realized what was happening. I wasn't sure what to do. Do I struggle? Do I fight? Do I try to run? What do I do? But he grabs me, and he's mumbling. 'Please son, please forgive me,' he says as he lays me down on top of the bundle of wood.

"I'm lying there, looking face up, seeing nothing but blue sky. Then I see him, a knife in his hand. He takes that knife, and then I feel the blade of the knife against my throat.

"I'll never forget the look on his face. It was twisted, awful, angry, in pain. It was horrific. He began to cut..." Ishmael was silent for a moment as felt the vein on the left side of his neck, where his skin still bore the knife scar, the only evidence outside of Ishmael's memories of that day.

"... and I began to bleed. And then, suddenly, he dropped the knife. He looked up, and behind him was a ram, bleating, caught in the weeds. He picked me up, and without even undoing those leather straps, he picked the ram up, and slit its throat. And set it all on fire."

Isaac put down his wine bowl. He held his hands up and looked at Ishmael.

"Sometimes, I can still feel the leather on my wrists, still binding me. I close my eyes and cannot help but see his face, his horrible face, looking at me as he raises the knife.

"I don't really know who I am angrier with. LORD, who asked my father to do that awful thing in the first place, or my father, who bargained with LORD to save an entire city but..." he choked up. "But wouldn't even speak up for me. His son."

He looked at Ishmael.

"You want that? You really want that?"

He tossed his wine bowl to the ground.

"You can have it. All of it. You are welcome to it."

Isaac stood up.

"And you know what angers me the most? When he was alive, we'd walk this valley, and people would whisper about us, 'There goes Abraham, beloved of LORD, friend of God, Abraham the faithful, the man who walks with God, the man of great and incredible faith! And what a blessing it must be to be his son!'"

He stumbled over to the tent door and opened it wide.

"You all admire him so damn much, you wretched people?!" he shouted, "You admire his faith? You love Abraham the Friend of God? You think he was a wonderful man? Well, try living with him! Try living with him!" he screamed, shaking his fist.

"Try..." his voice trailed off. "Try being his son."

Isaac was clearly drunk. Ishmael poured himself some more wine and sat up.

"Amen," he said, raising his wine bowl, taking a long drink. "No one knows what it means to be a son of Abraham. No one. They have no idea. Cast away. Abandoned. Sacrificed to the alleged 'glory' of God. It's a burden no one should carry."

In that moment, Isaac felt his blood stir to anger at Ishmael's words. What does he know? How could he even compare their lives? He looked cold and hard at his brother. But something in him – he wasn't sure what – held him to his cushion. Kept him silent. And he heard the wisdom in what Ishmael had just said. And like a soft rain falling on dry earth, it slowly began to sink into him. Whatever their differences, they shared the same pain.

"Amen," he said softly.

The two men sat silently, drinking wine, not looking at each other. Finally, Isaac spoke.

"You, you were the lucky one. He sent you away. You never had to live with him, to live with that crazy man who had raised a knife to slice your throat. After that, I never talked to him any more than I had to. When I told mother, something inside of her seemed to go out. They didn't even argue about it. There was just a deep sadness in her eyes. She never really spoke to him again either. A year later, she was dead.

"He broke her heart, I think. In the end, he killed her."

He picked up his wine bowl and shook it. He looked at, astonished in his drunkenness that his bowl was empty.

"Damn. I need more wine."

Ishmael grabbed a wineskin and filled Isaac bowl. Isaac took a long drink.

"Can we feed that rotten old bastard's dried up carcass to the vultures and the jackals? Or can we set him on fire? Because between the two of us, I suspect we can muster enough anger and hate to set all of Canaan on fire."

Ishmael laughed and shook his head.

"I was wrong to envy you, little brother."

* * *

Isaac awoke with a pounding in his head. It had been a long time since he'd drunk that much wine. He rose slowly and looked at his sleeping wife in the faint early dawn light, listening to her breathe. He loved her, and on days like this, days that promised to be long and difficult, he loved even more than he could express. Her smile, her laugh, her beautiful brown eyes, but mostly her gentle soul, were a comfort. Life had been hard – perhaps not as hard as Ishmael's – but Rebekah, his "Little Lamb," made the world a whole lot less unpleasant a place.

The eastern sky was just beginning to grow bright, a sliver of orange tight and flat on the horizon, and the slaves of Isaac's camp were stirring, getting ready to milk the goats and sheep, to make the day's bread, to gather the day's water from the nearby well. Isaac rose to wash, to get ready for prayer. He and Ishmael washed without exchanging words, and the slaves joined them for morning prayers, filling the air with chanting and incense.

After a breakfast of yogurt, honey, and dates, Isaac and Ishmael prepared for the day's business of burying their father. Isaac grabbed a pitcher of water while Ishmael grabbed a bag from his tent, and the two walked to the tent where Abraham lay.

"I brought spices, ointment, and myrrh. The finest from Yemen, little brother," Ishmael said. He reached into his bag and pulled out a big, round thing. It was rough and uneven, and full of holes. Isaac had never seen anything like it.

"A sponge from the Red Sea! It's for washing!" Ishmael

said. He squeezed it and laughed.

Isaac opened the tent flap and they entered. There he was. The man, who had in life been so fearsome and vibrant, who loomed over everything and everyone, whose eyes seemed at times betray a hint of madness, whose voice was sometimes mistaken as the voice of God by those who didn't know any better, lay there, on a simple wooden table. Silent, cold, lifeless.

The two men stood there for a moment looking at him. Feeling awkward. It had been two sunsets since he died, and they couldn't wait any longer, but an invisible hand held them back. This was their father. Whatever they may have felt about him, they were still in awe of him.

And still utterly terrified.

Ishmael took a breath.

"Little brother, we've both done this before. We've each buried a lot of men and women. This is no different." He looked at Isaac standing next to him. "This is the way of things. Sons bury fathers."

Isaac nodded. He had no words.

Ishmael moved first, approaching the table where Abraham lay. He removed the shroud and set his bag on the ground. Both men were startled by their father's nakedness. It reminded each of them of the uncomfortable memory when, to fulfill another strange command of LORD, Abraham had taken a knife to each boy and sliced off his foreskin.

"That hurt for days," Isaac said, shaking a little. Ishmael laughed slightly and nodded in agreement.

Isaac took a cloth, and Ishmael the sponge, and they slowly began to wash the old man's body. At the beginning, Isaac felt that this was something of a sacrilege, that he was somehow defiling the body of this amazing, terrible man who had been God's own friend, who had entertained angels and bargained with God to spare the souls of Sodom's damned denizens.

But as he washed Abraham's fingers, and arms, and toes, Isaac suddenly felt a peace he'd never felt before. As if this washing of his dead father was an act of worship. He suddenly felt close to this man, close in his death in a way he could never be in life. There was an intimacy to this washing, a tenderness he was able to show, and things he simply could never have said while Abraham still drew breath.

And so, Isaac was startled and a little disappointed when they were done. Ishmael reached down into his bag and pulled out some bottles and a bolt of white cloth.

"Egyptian linen, the best there is," he said, setting it aside. "Not even Pharaoh wears such linen."

They covered his body with the oil, and then began to wrap him. Each limb, and then the whole body. And as they went, they used more oil, and some of the spice pouches Ishmael brought. It took most of the morning, but finally, Abraham was wrapped from head to toe.

And Isaac found the smell wonderful. Intoxicating. An odd extravagance for the dead, he thought, who cannot appreciate this.

"I'll go get the oxcart," he told Ishmael.

After he returned, the two brothers loaded the old man's tightly wrapped corpse into the cart. Eleazar, Abraham's long-time servant and now himself a very old man, struggled into the driver's seat. Eleazar flicked the whip and the oxen started out, Isaac and Ishmael walking slowly behind the cart. Rebekah fell in right behind them, and behind her, many of their slaves.

Some wept openly. Some cried silently. Eleazar sat silently driving the cart, with tears in his eyes. Rebekah held tight to her veil, no sound from behind the black that obscured her face.

Only Isaac and Ishmael betrayed no emotion.

As the cortege wound its way through the countryside, they were joined by farmers and servants. It took an hour or so for the mourners, still mostly silent, to make their way through the countryside, a long, bedraggled, plodding train of humanity.

The real mourning, the weeping and the wailing, only really began when they got to Hebron. The people seemed to know what was coming, and as the parade following Isaac, Ishmael and the oxcart began weaving its way through town, women came out of their houses, men set down their tools and stopped working, children stopped running around playing, and they all stood and watched. Some bowed their heads, many began to wail and tear at their tunics. And many began falling in behind, joining the marchers as they made their way to the cave of Machpelah.

Isaac had only sort of expected this. But looking over at Ishmael, he could see his older brother was uncertain what to make of it all.

"I don't entirely understand either," he told Ishmael as he leaned over to talk above the noise.

The two said nothing as they made their way through town. Hebron was a small village, crossed quickly. It was not far to the cave.

Isaac looked back. It seemed like the entire town and much of the surrounding countryside, was following.

Near the mouth of the cave, the column stopped. Eleazar started to dismount the oxcart, but Isaac motioned to him to stay. Hands and bodies of the family's slaves and town residents came forth to help carry the body. At first, Isaac sighed with exasperation. "I don't *want* any help with this," he said to himself. Ishmael looked at him, uncertain, and then at the crowd. He nodded, and four men came forward. The six lifted Abraham's corpse – Isaac was shocked at how light his father's body had become – and hauled him gently and carefully into the cave.

"We can take it from here," Isaac said as they lay him next to the pile of bones and rags that had once been his mother.

The two men prayed. And found themselves overwhelmed. Isaac closed his eyes.

After leaving the cave, some local men plugged the entrance again, to keep the bodies safe. Mourners gathered, many kneeling, and praying. Isaac and Ishmael did as well and said the prayers they were supposed to say – the prayers their father had taught them – on the day the dead were interred.

Isaac wasn't sure how long he and Ishmael knelt there. He got up and touched his brother on the shoulder.

"We should go," he said.

Ishmael was still praying. He touched his forehead to the ground when he finished, and then stood up.

"Are you sure? Everyone is still praying?"

Isaac looked around.

"That's okay. He belongs to them now."

* * *

It had been quite a feast, and everyone was so full of roast lamb and wine and so sleepy that the camp was unusually quiet that afternoon. Only the young shepherds were stirring, trying to stay awake under the hot summer sun. Several were propped up under trees, barely paying any attention to the sheep in their charge.

But by late afternoon, life had returned to the camp. A young shepherd led Ishmael and Nebaioth's camels out, where the two sojourners looked them over to make sure everything was in order. Isaac stood watching them.

"Are you sure you can't stay any longer?"

Ishmael shook his head.

"I have to meet the rest of my caravan on the other side of the River Jordan, not far from Jericho. As it is, we've lost a couple of days on this trip. I have developed a reputation for punctuality, and I like to keep it."

Ishmael and his son mounted their camels and flicked their reins, commanding both animals to rise.

Isaac looked up at his older brother.

"So, will I ever see you again?"

Ishmael smiled.

"I don't know. I come this way a few times a year, and nothing says I can't stop by every now and again and say hello. And you should come south and see us sometime."

Isaac looked down at the ground.

"You know, I'm not much of a traveler. That was father's life. It's not mine."

"Okay. So, I'll come to see you."

The two men were silent.

"You know," Ishmael said. "You really are the child of promise."

Isaac looked up him. What? This again?

"And I told you. You can have it."

Ishmael leaned forward on the pommel of his saddle. He looked off toward the horizon, toward the hills.

"You know, LORD has never spoken to me, not like he spoke to dad," he said to Isaac.

"He's never spoken to me either," Isaac replied. With some bitterness in his voice.

"Let me finish, little brother. But LORD spoke to my mother about me, was the one who gave me my name, and told her to go back to Sarah, to 'submit' to her. LORD actually said I would be quite a troublemaker, and maybe I have been. At any rate, when Abraham finally sent me away, LORD spoke to him about me. At least that's what Abraham told me later."

He shifted slightly in his saddle.

"I would be a great people also. I am to be the father of many! Ornery desert people! Because I am a son of Abraham. But the word that matters here, little brother, is 'also.' The first promise, those LORD gave to our father so long ago, are for you. They aren't for me, as much as I wish they were.

"And for the first time in my life, I'm glad for you. Truly. For a long time, I'd wanted them to be my promises. I wanted to be something other than an afterthought."

He looked away. And then back at his brother, who stood there silently.

"I don't know if you will ever enjoy those promises, but they are for you. They are yours. Take some comfort in them. And as silent as LORD has been to you, little brother, it may be now that our father sleeps the sleep of the ages, that maybe LORD will see fit will speak. And then maybe those promises will really, truly become yours."

With that Ishmael raised his right hand smiled broadly at his brother Isaac.

"Little brother, LORD bless you and keep you, LORD make his face to shine upon you and be gracious to you, LORD lift up his face to you and give you peace. Amen."

"Amen," Isaac said silently. "And also with you."

With that, Ishmael and Nebiaoth began to ride away, their camels making a slow but steady trot. Isaac stood there, watching his brother and his nephew disappear into the distance.

He sat on his hillside that evening to watch the sunset. It still moved him, this setting of the sun. The sky went from orange to crimson to purple to black. The sky filled with stars, and he looked up at the dome, at the great backbone of night filling the sky. It looked like a great spill of milk, a stream cutting through the desert, God's seed dribbling out of the womb of the sky.

Or maybe a gash. Or a great wound. Perhaps it was all of these things. All of them at the same time.

Isaac sat in the darkness. All of this is mine now, *all of it*, including the promises. Those ridiculous promises LORD made. What does that even mean? How can they be mine if they were made to Abraham? And will LORD ever tell me?

"Will LORD ever tell me?" he asked again. Over and over.

He didn't know. He wondered how he would know. He wondered how long he would have to wait to know. Days? Months? Years? A whole lifetime?

But what else did Isaac have but waiting? So, as he beheld the darkened sky full of stars, he decided he would wait. LORD most certainly had not abandoned him. How could he? Not after all this.

He would wait.

The Undead // Charles Featherstone

The first thing he noticed was the smell.

He couldn't quite put his finger on what it was. It felt heavy, damp, and musty even. It wasn't unpleasant, but he'd rather not smell it all the same. Breathing wasn't an option, of course, but he wondered how long it would take to get used to that smell.

And it was dark, too. Dark. Warm, not hot and humid, but not wet. The air wasn't moving either.

Wait, it wasn't dark. He just hadn't opened his eyes. He opened them. Nope, it was still dark. He sat up, looked around. Goodness, but it was dark. He looked down, moved his legs a bit. Nope, still there, still working. He held out his hands, wriggled his finger. Nope, these still work too.

Everywhere, there was a kind-of greenish light. It didn't seem to come from anywhere, and so his shadow – his anti-green shadow – was cast all around him, a circle of semi-shadow that ringed him.

He struggled to stand up. He looked around. There was no horizon, no terrain, nothing definable. The only way he could tell up from down is that he was standing on something.

But what? Soil? Rock? He couldn't tell.

Somewhere, away, he saw forms moving. He could hear whispering. No much, just a little.

"Hello? Hello? Is there anyone here?"

There was no echo. That unnerved him.

"Hello? Hello? Is there anyone here?"

Nothing.

Out of the corner of his eye, he noticed something moving. A shadow. He turned to it, and ran. It was a man, or rather, it looked like a man, but it didn't. Light shone through it, and the form didn't seem to notice him.

"I am Korah, son of Izhar, son of Kohath! Who are you? Where am I?"

"Hmm? Who am I? I'm not sure. I think my name is Cain. That's what I was called." The form looked at Korah with deep pity in its eyes. "You shouldn't be talking here. This is a place of silence. I must go. I must... wander."

The form walked away. Korah tried to stop it, tried blocking it, but the shadowy form just walked right through him.

Korah turned and watched the form walk away.

"Where am I? WHERE AM I?"

"I believe I can help you with that."

Korah turned again. Before him stood a frightening visage – a form, wrapped in a heavy black tunic, face only half-visible. All he could see was a the chin and jaw of a very pale face. And those eyes, bright yellow eyes glowing in the darkness.

Glowing like coals in a fire.

"Who... who are you?"

"I am Abaddon, the keeper of this place. You, Korah, son of Izhar, son of Kohath, are in Sheol, the place of the dead. The place farthest from God. The place where God is not."

Korah felt his heart skip a beat.

"I'm ... I'm dead?"

"You must be, if you are here. No one but the dead come to this place."

There was silence. Korah felt his heart pounding, in the silence of the place heard his breathing as if were a roaring thunder storm.

"But you don't ... you don't seem dead." Abaddon put out a bony, pale hand and touched Korah's arm, stroked it softly, and then placed that hand on his chest.

Korah noticed the hand felt cold. The only cold thing in this place.

39

"Nope, you aren't dead. You are not dead at all. That is very odd. You should not even be here."

"Then how do I get out? How do I get back?"

"I don't know. This has never happened before. I don't know what to do." Abaddon lowered his hand. "I'm at a loss. Occasionally a spirit will be summoned above by a sorcerer or a medium, but those are the souls of those already dead. No one has ever come down here alive before. I have no idea how to get you back above."

Korah looked around. He was feeling panic coming on.

"Is there a path, or a trail, or caves that go up... to the land above? I mean, how do you get there?"

"I don't go above. There's no reason to. So I don't know if there's a path. Honestly. There may be one, but I don't know. Well, I have the dead to attend to."

And suddenly Abaddon was gone.

Korah looked around. Now he was panicking. How had he gotten here? Oh, right, suddenly he remembered. He'd led a rebellion against Moses in the wilderness. And Moses called upon the ground to open and swallow him, he and all his followers.

And it had. And he, and all those who had followed him in his challenge to Moses, were here. Which meant he was not alone! Somewhere, out there, were the others, alive like him! Which meant he was not alone.

Maybe they could work together and find a way out.

* * *

Korah quickly found most of his followers. Abaddon helped a bit with this, both amused and a little concerned that his domain was suddenly filled with people who were not dead. They set up camp on a flat plain hosting two thin, giant vertical rocks, using spare articles of clothing to fashion crude shelters.

Their eyes grew accustomed to the semi-darkness, and they began to make out features. A few distorted scrub plants. The sand was fine, black, and smooth to the touch. There was no water.

No water. It meant they would go thirsty. And hungry.

"Abaddon!" Korah called out. The master of this place usually came when Korah called his name. "Abaddon, where are you?!"

It took a moment. But the heavily shrouded figure appeared.

"Settling in?"

"No, we are not!" Korah angrily replied. "What are we supposed to do for food and drink? There's no water here, and nothing to eat. We will all starve!"

Korah thought he almost saw a smile on that darkened face.

"Then you will be dead and you will truly belong here," Abaddon replied.

And he sighed, something Korah had never heard before. "There is no water here. And no food. The others here – *the dead* – don't need such things. So, I do not know what to tell you. Best of luck, though."

The living inmates of Sheol quickly discovered, however, that they didn't get hungry. And they didn't get thirsty. They didn't even seem to get tired, though they could sleep if they chose. But it was always a restless, dreamless, troubled sleep. It was as if they weren't quite alive anymore, but weren't quite yet dead either.

It didn't help matters that Sheol was dark and flat, a land nearly devoid of landmarks. It was easy to get lost, or walk in circles. After a while, they gave up looking for a way out. There was too much Sheol. Simply too much.

There was no weather, no rain, no snow, no hot, no cold. No elements they needed protecting from.

And time, well, there was no way to mark time in Sheol. There were no days, no nights, no months, no seasons, no years. Just time, endless time, time together. Korah and his people were slowly being driven – and driving each other – to madness, and one by one, the living wandered away, to seek solitude, seek the company of the silent dead who paid them no attention.

Korah sat alone, on a big black rock he long ago claimed as his home. He sat alone in thought. His thoughts were all he had left.

A shadow walked past. He recognized it. Moses!

He got up and ran to it.

"You! I remember you! Do you remember me? Do you see where you've gotten me? Look at what you did! Look at me! Look at me see! A living, breathing man, condemned to an eternal life in this place of the dead!"

The shadow of Moses looked past him. And kept walking.

"That's nice," it said absentmindedly, lost in thought.

Korah didn't even have the strength and desire to go after Moses. He meandered back to his rock and sat down.

"Death," he said, weeping. "Death, please come for me. Please take me."

It never came. It never ever came.

* * *

Korah, however, saw the dead come, the dead of Israel, of Egypt, of places he'd never heard of when he lived on Earth. They came, and came, and came. And they never really listened to Korah, never really spoke to him, never considered him, never showed any interest in him.

Ages alone. Of loneliness. This, Korah said to himself, was worse than death. Death is non-existence, obliteration, nothingness. The souls here seem to know they are dead, but they don't feel their death. They don't feel anything. But I feel everything! My heart still beats, my skin still senses everything, my eyes still see, my ears hear, my tongue and my nose taste and smell! But there is nothing is feel here, nothing to sense. This is a living death, all this nothingness felt and tasted and smelled.

"Abaddon," he asked softly once. "How long have I been here?"

"How long? Hmmm, as it is reckoned by the Egyptians, you have been here for exactly 1,349 years?"

Korah sighed.

"Is that long?"

Abaddon didn't look at him.

"There is no long here. No short here. There is just time, unmeasured."

It was far longer than Korah could even begin to know.

Then *he* came. He was different. He was not a shadow. He had a flesh and blood body, just like Korah's. It was bruised and bloody, something horrific had happened to him. And he saw Korah. And spoke to him.

"The peace and blessings of God Almighty be with you, Korah, son of Izhar, son of Kohath!"

Korah was startled. He wasn't sure he was capable of being startled after all this time. He'd never heard such words said in this place. Not in all the time he'd been here. No one ever blessed God, or even spoken his name, here in Sheol.

"You... you spoke to me! You see me!"

"Yes, I see you. I am here for you. To redeem you."

Korah looked at the man in amazement.

"Are... are you dead?"

"I am. I died about five hours ago."

Hours. Days. Years. Words Korah had not heard in a long, long time.

"But... but how? You have a body, a flesh and blood like mine. The dead here are only shadows."

The man smiled. It had been an aeon since Korah had smiled himself, much less even seen one.

"It is more than I can tell you now. Just know that I am the one who comes to deliver you from this place. Do you believe that?"

Korah fell on his knees.

"If you are here to deliver me, then you could only be God

Almighty himself!"

The man's smile got wider.

"Korah, son of Izhar, son of Kohath, your sins are forgiven. And now, I give you the gift of death. For no one I have met needs death as much as you."

Korah felt a tightness in his chest, and it quickly overwhelmed him. Everything went truly black. He suddenly he stood next to the man, and was now a shadow, unfeeling, unconcerned, uncaring, looking at his own body, lying crumpled on the dark sand.

He saw the hooded figure of Abaddon.

"I wish I could have done that."

The man grew serious.

"But he's not yours. He's mine. I'm taking him with the others, and we're leaving this place."

The man touched Korah's shadow, and suddenly he could feel, he could think, he could perceive. He was still dead, but he also something else now too. Something that didn't make sense.

"Will I be alone? Will you come back for me?" Abaddon's voice was almost pathetic.

"You will be alone for a time. But I promise, I will come back for you. I will not leave you here."

The hooded figure was gone. Korah looked at the man.

"Who are you?"

The man smiled again.

"That's a long story, my friend," he said, putting his arm around the shadow that was Korah. "Come, follow me, and I will tell you all about it..."

Laced // Malcolm Himschoot

Who is in? Who is out? Who decides? Who is the foreigner?

***

She laced up, for the thousandth time since leaving home, the crimson cords of her sandals. The walk was hot and dusty, as expected. Her sandals were suited to the purpose, the soles well-worn, the fabric ties easily adjusted. With a coating of dust her ankles did not sweat. Each footfall met dirt soft or firm.

An evening sun cast evening upon her path, its light gleaming and striking a contrast upon the stark desert rocks at roadside and the barren troughs of desert irrigation. Signs everywhere of how hard the earth could be and just how quick a drought could take a crop. With every change, a migration of animals and people followed water and food.

Not many years before, the woman Ruth now traveled with was only a stranger to her. Naomi was her name then, before she chose to call herself nothing but bitterness and emptiness. Mara was her name now. She came by this same road but the other way, from her homeland to Ruth's.

Mara had come with her family. Back then. When she had family. Just as Ruth was migrating now, Mara's family was migrating then. Led by famine, pushed by drought, thirsting for their own survival, they had come, none of them knowing if their stay would be short and temporary or long and permanent. They relied upon strangers. If they found a well, they drank. If they found peace, they rested. If they found violence, they kept going.

Mara's people found hospitality. Since Ruth's people lived by the law of the wilderness. Next time it could be you in search of a home, in search of water, in search of food and in search of survival. They knew it could be you starting over and needing safety. Ruth's people married Mara's people, so the two families became one.

Ruth had been married to Kilion, the younger son. She and Kilion learned each other's language, and often had conversations to compare the sense of things, food, and traditions of the in-laws. They had conversations about the stars and seasons, amulets and rituals, clothes and gender, names and destinies, scars and wardrobe. For instance, the sandals she was wearing now. Not home-made but procured by Kilion at the town market. Ruth, carrying all she owned in a basket atop her head, stopped to adjust the laces once more.

After sunset, Ruth and Mara found themselves in a position they never would have been in, if Kilion and the others were still living. Women on the road to Judah, unaccompanied by men, women conspicuously alone, huddled in the dark off to one side, no shelter there and no one to take them in. Marauding animals, malicious humans, could take advantage. The nighttime sky turned eery – not like at home. Longing for home, in fear of this harsh and dreadful night, a third woman had already turned back. Orpah – Ruth's sister-in-law, widow of Mahlon.

The two women proceeded, one dusty footstep after the other. Ruth tried not to think what would come next. What she was prepared to do or spend or deal or divest in order to build a new life for herself and Mara. She knew how others who found themselves in her situation ended up selling sex and using their body to survive. Would days turn into months and months into years? Would she have a choice? Would she ever be able to do anything else? Word got around, after all.

* * *

Word was, Naomi was returning to Bethlehem. With a foreigner.

Boaz waited there, a Bethlehemite who worked a field, bartered in town, and enjoyed a man's prerogative to be married or not. This particular morning he laced up his sandals, prepared for another day's work. He didn't have any way of knowing that his relatives had died in Moab. He wasn't aware of any particular possibilities or obligations as a "kinsman redeemer" to a deceased relative. He was unaware of how his family life was about to change.

What he did know was the law that God commanded in Torah:

> *"When you reap the harvest of your land, you shall not reap to the very edges of your field, or gather the gleanings of your harvest. You shall not strip your vineyard bare, or gather the fallen grapes of your vineyard; you shall leave them for the poor and the alien: I am the Lord your God."*

He lived by it.

> *"When a stranger resides with you in your land, you shall not wrong him. The stranger who resides with you shall be to you as one of your citizens; you shall love him as yourself, for you were strangers in the land of Egypt: I the Lord am your God."*

Such scripture Boaz had known ever since he was a boy in lessons. On this day, like every day, he was reminded of the law, and also the part of the law that said a male relative must redeem – acquire – the surviving female spouse of a relative. Else she, like the slaves and the immigrants, would go poor and hungry.

Ruth showed up, hungry but hiding it and desperate but denying it. It happened to be Boaz's field she chose to glean, gathering up the grain left behind by the harvesters of the barley as they gathered it into sheaves. At breaktime Boaz called to her, among all the raggedy weeds and skinny scraps of beggars in the heat. He told her, "Help yourself to some water, let me know if anyone harasses you." Ruth realized he was taking an interest. She realized she would have something to eat. That night, while Boaz spoke with the village elders to find out more about her, Ruth went with quick steps back to her mother-in-law's house.

Mara was no fool. The first thing she wanted to know was, who was this man. Who were his people? What was his lineage? She found out, and made her prediction the next day.

The morning after Ruth went to Boaz at the threshing floor, lied down with him where he was sleeping, took his clothes off and impressed upon his old body her young one.

Ruth returned to Naomi in the wee hours of the morning, before anyone but the goatherds was awake. Had they been awake they would have seen. Whatever it was they would have seen. Was it shame? Or, self-preservation?

Naomi received her, put a grip with both her hands on Ruth's shivering shoulders, and said to her, "Just wait. Don't worry. He'll arrange to marry you. Right away."

Boaz did as she predicted. He went right to the rich men to arrange it. Marriage wasn't usually a law applicable to foreigners. But there was no reason it shouldn't be. Women were property, after all, and Ruth had been the property of a citizen. So he had the documents drawn up – or the equivalent. He unlaced the cords of his ruddy sandal and handed it over, as sealed and binding as any fingerprint.

Thus was Ruth transferred into Boaz' name, and her children into his line.

Witnesses watched the proceedings. They agreed to the deal and more than that, they pronounced it sacred. No longer was Ruth a foreigner in their midst, they actually asked their God's blessings upon her. They said, "May God make this woman who is coming into your household like Rachel and Leah – who built our family, who built up our tribe, without whom none of us would be here. May God make your children from this woman like the children who came before us and who became our ancestors. May we together be more through the years, because of her!"

Prophets, they were who said these things! Prophets according to the bards who wrote the story of the birth of Christ: son of David, son of Jesse, son of Obed, son of Boaz, all those years ago.

* * *

It's a complicated family tree, the outsiders getting mixed up with the insiders. And the telling of it gets even more complicated: Where did Boaz come by his openness to relationship with the foreigner?

Was it because Boaz was a good man, a kind man, benevolent, moral, legal and upstanding? Would he be listed with the charitable philanthropists of his day? Maybe. That's the way the story is usually told. But it might surprise us to learn that no citizen had begun the turn of events that led to this day of celebrative inclusion. No benevolent judge with all the power of the government conferred leniency. No majority decided to be tolerant. No people in privilege passed a policy.

Well, they did. They did eventually, with the passing of the red-laced sandal in the town square as a marital transaction.

But that's not where this story started. This story started with a thoroughly marginalized woman who worked in the world's oldest profession.

I mean Boaz's mother.

Rahab. The foreigner. Rahab, the Canaanite. Rahab, the prostitute.

A generation before Ruth's story, it was Rahab who received two Israelites into her home, her place of work, her brothel. Two young male soldiers. Then, she hid them for safety when she learned they were spies. Rahab let them out of the wall of the city of Jericho when it was dangerous by tying a certain cord to her window. When they saw that cord later, she made them promise they would remember her during their armed campaign, and not wipe out her family.

The cord identifying Boaz's mother that fateful night was scarlet.

The color of sex, the color of daring, the color of blood and passion and risk, and trespass, and life.

A scarlet cord links our heroines across the generations, whose story continues to unite the marginalized, the displaced, the dislocated, the disreputable, the daring, the determined, the faithful, the prophetic, and the creators of a way forward, with God's help.

Laced together by that scarlet lifeline - however bodies or spirits are threatened, used or misused - do not give out, do not give up. Rahab taught Boaz, and Boaz heard it again from Ruth:

"We do not give into voices of humiliation, alienation, oppression, or depression. We survive. We prevail."

From Rahab to Ruth. From Ruth to David. From David to Jesus. The first chapter of the New Testament, binding heaven and earth through the lineage of an incarnate God, tells this truth. The story that set in motion a Christian people was set in motion by one whose life was lived in the porous boundary of a wall.

This side, that side, did it ultimately matter? People would cross. People would come in. People would go out. The climate would change. Jobs would dry up. Children had to eat.

If ever one had tried to prevent risk by ousting the foreigner, now was not that time. It was time to claim the law of survival, the law of the desert, the law of hospitality, the wisdom of the trickster and a queer part of liberation, which is all the same thing, which is this. You can't benefit by turning someone away and denying you're related. You, them, you're all in it together. You're in the land together, and your best bet in the land is to create relationships. The kind to ensure that the one you looked down on yesterday as a 'foreigner' will not have any motive tomorrow to do the same to you.

My Name is Job // Kathryn Muyskens

They were stuck in traffic, pure deadlock. Eli, Bill and Zach, college buddies, were trying to begin their daytrip to go hiking in the mountains. But, it seemed like everyone had the same idea that weekend, and they were going nowhere fast.

Eli noticed a homeless man on the side of the road. He walked slowly down the side of the gridlocked cars, holding a sign that read, "My name is Job, but I can't get one."

Eli thought the sign was clever. Bill, who was driving, noticed the homeless man too, and quickly pressed the lock button on the car doors.

"Why did you do that?" Eli asked.

"Come on, what do you mean, 'why?'" Bill said dismissively, "It's the smart thing to do."

The homeless man was a bit unsavory looking, but Eli didn't think he looked dangerous. If anything he looked more like he had been chewed up and spit out by danger a long time ago and had never truly recovered.

Job, if that was his real name, looked about sixty. His hair was matted, grizzled and sparse. And his face was a leathery brown mask of wrinkles. But, his eyes peered out of that mask with a surprising liveliness.

Job stopped by the window of one of the cars ahead of them and accepted a few dollars from the driver.

"Roll down the window, he's coming our way," Eli said.

"No, man, what are you thinking? He's just going to use anything you give him to buy drugs or alcohol. That's what they all say," Zach chimed in.

"You really think he looks like the partying type?" Eli asked, "He's so old and frail looking."

"Yeah, and if you give him money, he's just going to use it to dig his own grave. How do you think he wound up homeless in the first place? When you don't have any self-discipline and you do stupid stuff, this is what happens."

"How can you possibly know that's why he's homeless?" Eli scoffed, "He could have been just like us once. He could be a perfectly nice guy."

"No way! Look at us, Eli, we're pretty 'together.' I mean, we all have decent grades; we're going to a decent school. You've got that job already. None of us gamble or anything like that. We're doing everything right. We are about to graduate. We've got everything going for us. This guy, he probably has some mental problems. Maybe he's just not that bright, or maybe he's got some huge addiction problem."

Job was nearing their car.

"Why don't we just ask him?" Eli suggested, "I mean, he's right there. We can just ask him and settle this once and for all."

"Isn't that kind of rude?" Bill asked uncomfortably.

"Isn't it kind of rude to just assume he's a drug addict?" Eli rolled down his window and stuck an arm out, waving to Job.

Job walked over, "Thank you. Anything helps," he said.

Eli felt a bit awkward, not sure how to begin the conversation, "Hey Job, I like your sign," he began, "I just have a couple questions for you."

"Okay," Job said in a dry and cracking voice, "Shoot."

Traffic was showing no signs of easing up, but Eli knew that could change in an instant, so he went straight to the point with his question, "How'd you wind up here, man? I mean, how'd you wind up homeless and all?"

"Bad luck, mostly."

"We were kind of hoping for a little more detail." Eli fished in his backpack for the lunch he'd packed, "I'll trade you. One life story for a sandwich, chips and a bottle of water? How's that sound?"

Job cracked a smile, "We ain't got enough time, son."

"Cliffnotes version then?"

Bill helped the conversation along, asking, "Like, what was your job before all this?"

"I was a chemical engineer."

"No kidding!" Eli exclaimed.

"No way... if you were really a chemical engineer, how can you be out of work now? That stuff is in demand, isn't it?"

"Yes, it is. But when I got cancer, I couldn't work any longer. I got a brain tumor. It started interfering with my ability to concentrate. I started forgetting things."

At the mention of cancer, an uneasy quiet settled in the car.

"Don't look so sad, boys," Job said in a jocular tone, "I lived. I'm fine now, just missing a bit of brain tissue." Job tapped the side of his head as he spoke and made a funny face, trying to lighten the mood. But Bill noticed the end of a scar peeking out from beneath the knotted hair on the man's scalp.

Bill tried to crack a smile, but he still felt awkward. He wanted to maintain his skepticism. After all, he didn't know this man, how did they know he wasn't making up this story to gain sympathy? "Being a chemical engineer is high paying work, right? Didn't you have savings?" he asked.

"Sure I did," Job said, "But medical bills burned through that pretty quickly."

"No insurance?"

"Not enough."

"No family? No one to turn to?"

Job's eyes glittered on his weathered face, "I used to have a family. But they've since passed away." Job had seemed happy enough to tell his story a moment before, but now his past seemed to be enveloping him. As he spoke, Eli got the sense that Job was getting farther and farther away, "There was a fire... I pretty much lost everything in that fire."

There was a long pause. Suddenly, the silence was broken by cars honking. A little space had opened up in front of their car.

Bill took his foot off the break and let the car inch forward. Job was left a couple feet behind, caught in a world of memory.

Eli poked his head out the window and called back to him, "Hey, Job."

Job seemed to snap out of his reverie then. He walked back to the open window.

"I'm sorry for bringing it all up," Eli said, "Here you go." He handed him the bagged lunch. But it somehow felt like a cheap gesture.

Job accepted the lunch, "God bless you."

"God?" Eli said, there was something jarring to him about the mention of God in such a situation, "You believe in God, Job?"

"Of course. Now more than ever."

Eli was puzzled. If anyone had a reason to reject the idea of God, he would have thought Job did.

Job noticed Eli's perplexed expression, "I was raised in a Christian home," he said.

"I was too. But wouldn't you feel angry at God for letting this all happen to you?" Eli asked. Before he had known Job was a Christian, Eli had thought the story was sad, but now it felt unjust as well. Eli had been taught all his life that God loved his followers. How could God let all this tragedy befall one of his own?

"God is not some divine vending machine," Job said, seeming to guess Eli's thoughts, "The Lord giveth, and He taketh away."

"Come on, that's just taking the easy way out," Bill couldn't restrain himself any longer, "You can't just blame God for everything. You have to control your life, you have to own your decisions. You're the reason you got here."

Job looked at Bill, but strangely didn't seem offended by his accusatory tone, "But that's just it, son. If there's one thing in life I've learned by now, it's that we don't have control. None of us do.

"All that we have, all that any of us have, we have by God's grace alone. There's no such thing as earning it, no such thing as deserving it. There's no such thing as certainty. There is only faith. And there's no such thing as control, there's only compassion."

"I don't know if I buy that," Bill said, and before Job could respond the traffic opened up. Bill stepped on the gas and the three friends were finally speeding along on their way to the mountains.

Job and his disturbing and unsettling story were left behind them on the road. Eli couldn't help one last look back. Job was facing away. Holding up his sign to the oncoming cars with one hand and holding Eli's lunch in the other.

* * *

That day in the mountains, unfolded much like any other. The three friends hiked to a high mountain lake. But Job's words had followed them all, and as they took in the fresh air and the scenery his voice seemed to hang in the air around them.

"You know, just the other day I couldn't wait for this trip," Zach said. He hadn't spoken much since the conversation with Job, "But now it feels different."

"How so?" asked Bill.

"Usually when we come out here, it feels like a break from the grind, you know? But now, it seems brighter somehow. I don't know why."

"I think I know what you mean," said Eli, "I usually feel like I deserve a vacation after all the work I do the rest of the time. But today, it just feels like a gift."

"I'm hungry. Let's eat lunch." Bill looked at the lunch he had packed. A steak sandwich he had made with care. He was hungry enough to eat it all. But he stopped himself. He offered half to Eli.

Eli nodded his thanks. Zach followed suit and offered him the chips he'd packed. They ate in silence, taking in the magnificent view before them. And each one of them privately felt a little humbled, a little sad, a little uncertain, but also overwhelmingly blessed.

The Gospel According to Us

Tomato Seeds // Emily Olsen

How have things been? Pretty much the same. Business is as it's always been: not great, but there. We all get paid and no one's died of food poisoning yet. Oh, you mean with me? Well, pretty much the same too.

Except for this one thing. Just a weird customer coming in and spooking me really. Who? Well, Harold said he saw him playing taps at that Memorial Day service over in Bentley last spring, but me and Earl didn't recognize him. The thing is, none of us saw him come in the door. None of us.

Us, of course, being me, Earl, and Harold. And Keith behind the grill, but he was making Earl's eggs and wouldn't have seen much of anything anyway. To be fair, Earl and Harold were facing the other direction. You know how they are. They've sat in those same booths at the restaurant since forever, the ones facing away from the door, so they can keep an eye on Keith and heckle him if need be. So I guess that leaves me, but I was pouring Earl's coffee and was looking at his mug while I did it. Spilling hot coffee on an 87 year-old man, even by accident, is no laughing matter.

"Is that deer head new?" Earl asked. As if the buck Keith shot last year had just wandered by and stuck its head through the wall.

"Been there since June, Earl." I said as I finished topping off his coffee.

"What?" Earl stuck his finger behind his ear and tried to turn up the volume on his hearing aid.

"It's not new!" I yelled.

"If you say so, but I never seen it before."

"That's because you face the grill and not the door, Earl!" hollered Harold. "If you turned around once in a while, maybe you'd be able to keep track of things around here."

"I keep track of things just fine" snapped Earl. "And don't pretend you knew that deer that was there, Harold. You're facing the same way I am."

"I don't know how long it's been here, but I'd say a deer head sticking out of a wall looks pretty stupid, especially when it's wearing a red Santa hat." The last remark hadn't come from

Harold, Earl, or Keith. A stranger, about Earl's vintage, was sitting alone in a booth on the other side of the restaurant. A walker was leaned up against the wall across from him. "Can a man get a cup of coffee around here?" he demanded.

"Oh, Ria's falling down on the job again" chortled Harold. "Man's probably been sitting there for hours."

"Been there since last night, I'll bet" Earl piped up. "Like the damn deer head."

I scrambled to grab a coffee mug, napkin, and coffee pot. "Good morning," I said, "would you like cream or sugar with that?"

"Just cream" he replied.

"He's gonna need a menu" remarked Earl.

"Watch out Ria, Earl's trying to do your job again!" warned Harold.

"Don't worry, Earl, I'm getting him one" I said as I hustled off to get a pitcher of cream and dig out a breakfast menu.

Well, of course we still have breakfast menus! It's just Earl and Harold never use the damn things. You know how mornings are at the restaurant: slow, sparse, and predictable. We usually only need the breakfast menus on the weekends and that day was a Tuesday.

Now, I know you're wondering how some old geezer with a walker could blow into the restaurant, shut that creaky door, and slip into a booth without any of us noticing. Truth is, your guess is as good as mine. I have no idea how he managed it. He didn't look particularly sneaky, just old and a little tired. Not that I was particularly sympathetic at the time.

To be honest, I was steaming a bit about the deer comment. Winter around here is so damned depressing and comes so fast, I really do try to make the restaurant as festive as possible, especially for the holidays. Earl, Harold, and the other folks who wander in for lunch or supper appreciate a bit of holly in December, a heart or two in February, and a gang of Leprechauns come March. If nothing else, it gives them something to talk about.

I don't need to tell you that this wasn't the first time that Earl had asked about the deer head. He tends to rediscover the thing at least once a month, to the delight of anyone else who happens to be hanging around. So let's just say I didn't appreciate this geezer coming into our restaurant and criticizing the decorations as if he owned the place. He didn't.

Yes, I know, Earl and Harold say whatever they want, whenever they want. But, you see, they've earned it. The two of them are practically family. They've shown up morning after morning, year after year, rain, shine, and power outage. If Earl doesn't come to breakfast, Keith, or me, or one of the other waitresses will call his house to make sure he hasn't gone and pitched off his porch. Same for Harold, but he lives with his daughter, who usually keeps an eye on him.

This geezer wasn't Earl or Harold. Maybe he was someone's grandpa come up to visit, or a great uncle with no grandkids of his own. Maybe his kids had brought him up with them to go ice fishing once the river got good and frozen. Whoever he was and wherever he was from, he wasn't familiar and I didn't like his attitude.

So, as you can imagine, I was a little abrupt in my service. I came back to his booth, plopped down the creamer and a menu without so much as a "how are you." I was about to head back to the kitchen to pick up Earl's eggs when the old guy reached out and grabbed my wrist.

"Hey Cutey-Pie." he said. "Let me talk to you for a sec."

Now, I know you're thinking that I should have been creeped out and told him to keep his hands to himself, but he was an old man, you see. He had a walker, for goodness sakes! Just because I had decided that I didn't like him, didn't mean I was afraid of him. He was obnoxious, sure, but most people are when they hit 80. Earl and Harold are a case in point. I may not have heard him come in, and he might have been irritating, but, as far as I could tell, the man was harmless.

"What do you need?" I asked.

"Did you put that stupid little hat on the deer?" he asked. "I should have realized, sweetheart. Deer or anyone else's heads sticking out of walls don't really do it for me, but I shouldn't have made fun of you. You done a good job prettying this place up. It looks like those boys over there really appreciate it."

"Thanks" I said. I hadn't expected an apology. Heck, I hadn't even told him the hat on the deer was my idea. I guess my face and my coolness toward him must have said a lot more than I realized.

"Now, sit down" the man motioned to the seat across from him. "Don't worry about the boys. They'll keep. I've got something important to tell you."

I probably should have just told him that I was busy or that I'd check on him later. I could have even ignored his request and asked him what he wanted for breakfast. I honestly don't know why I sat down. True, I appreciated his apology. I'm fond of Earl and Harold, but the two of them wouldn't know an apology if it served them breakfast. But more than that, the man looked urgent. It seemed like he had something really important to say and I was the only one on hand to hear it. If I've learned one thing from having Earl and Harold troop in for breakfast year after year, it's that you've got to humor these older folks. When they have something to say, it's best to let them say it.

The man beamed as I sat down. I mean, he lit up, that's the only way that can describe it. His eyes shone and he let me get a good, long look at his immaculately clean dentures. "It's so good to meet you, Ria."

"Do I know you?" I asked.

"Everyone knows everyone around here" he said, taking in the restaurant with a wave of his arm. He was right about that, you know. In a small town with an even smaller gene pool, even if you don't recognize someone, you probably know her cousin or sister-in-law pretty well. Or, come to think of it, he might have just heard Earl or Harold hollering for me.

"Who are you then?"

"Don't worry about me, Cutey-Pie" the man reached across the table and took my hand and before I could pull away, or do anything, really, he launched into what he had to say, "I've got important news for you, Cutey-Pie!" he exclaimed. "Amazing news! News that would make that deer leap off the wall and go tearing through the state forest."

"Without any legs?" The old man gave me a withering look. "Sorry," I said, "let's hear this news."

"Ria," the man looked right into my eyes, "you're going to have a baby!"

"Excuse me?"

"You, Ria, you're gonna have a baby boy!"

What made him say that? Damned if I know. I don't have a sweetie right now. Keith's taken me down to the city to see a movie a couple times, but that was months ago and you know how things are anyway. It's not as if I have the spare time to go running around getting pregnant. With waitressing, and my job at the daycare, and of course those night classes I'm taking, I barely have time to sleep by myself, let alone with anyone else. And there's the pill of course. I may take it mostly to keep the zits away, but it keeps away the babies too, if you know what I mean.

What I'm saying is, the geezer had no idea what he was talking about. Not that I was particularly concerned at that point. The man was probably just a little off his rocker. It happens sometimes.

What? People going crazy? Yes, that, but more specifically, people going crazy and wandering into the restaurant. We've all had our share of walky-talkies to deal with over the last couple years. For instance, there was the lady who kept trying to eat the plastic lettuce leaves we use to pretty up the salad bar. Earl and Harold got a real kick out of that. Then there was the guy who always ordered pancakes for his deceased wife. An omelet for him and pancakes for poor Shirley. He never ate the pancakes, just ordered them, paid for them, and left a tip once he had finished his omelet. We never could figure out what to do with the damn pancakes when he left.

You get them around here, the walky-talkies. There's something about the smell of food and the sound of voices that just kind of draws them. They're harmless for the most part too. So I figured that the man was just another nutcase off his meds and out to lunch, or breakfast, as the case may be. He'd probably wandered out the door when his kids were distracted and meandered down the road to pay us a visit. Fine, I thought, let me just keep him talking until his kids realize he's missing. They'll probably call around the town before bringing in the cops, and then we'll let them know that grandpa's right here, safe and sound, and they'll come pick him up. Easy. We may even get a nice tip for feeding him breakfast and keeping him safe.

"Tell me," I said "how is this all going to work?"

"Well, the way it always works, Cutey-Pie," he explained. "You're gonna get pregnant and then nine months later, here comes the baby!"

Just what I needed: sex-ed from a batty old man. If I kept on going, he was probably going to start talking about flowers, bees, and pollination, or whatever nonsense they're using these days to avoid telling twelve year-olds about sex.

"Okay, that makes sense, but who's going to be the baby's daddy?"

"There won't be a daddy, so to speak," the geezer took a sip of his coffee before continuing, "just the Holy Spirit."

"I beg your pardon?"

"The Holy Spirit, Cutey-Pie. The Holy Spirit's gonna overshadow you and the power of the most high's gonna come upon you and as a direct result your baby's gonna be holy."

"Weird."

Now, don't look at me like that. What else could I say? It would be one thing if he'd gone all fortune teller on me and predicted a dark and handsome stranger in my future, but this was just plain odd. Overshadow? What did that even mean? And how could a baby be holy? I've seen my fair share of babies at the daycare. They scream, they shit all over the place, and they refuse to fall into any sort of workable schedule. There is nothing holy about them. They're just babies.

"Don't worry, Cutey-Pie" the geezer patted my hand, "the mechanics of the thing are a little beyond the both of us. Just know that you're gonna get a pretty darnn wonderful gift."

Gift. That's what he said. As if babies were just little accessories that people used to decorate their lives. A bike when you turn nine, high heels when you're 13, and a baby when you're 20 so we all know who's making it in this town.

I couldn't help it. I knew the man was crazy with his talk of babies and holy spirits, but I was mad. How dare he hand me a lifetime of trouble like it was a pair of shoes.

"I don't want your gift." I stated.

"It's not-"

"No, I don't want it, or him for that matter. Listen to me, I have a life. It's not perfect, it's not easy, but it's mine. I don't need a baby to make it better. A baby would probably make it harder, to be honest. If I want a baby I'll have one on my terms, not yours." I started to slide out of the booth. Maybe Keith had gotten a call from this guy's family and we'd be able to hand him off. If not, I was calling the cops. He was crazy and making me uncomfortable. I was done.

"It's not just your gift, you know." The old man leaned back in his seat and looked up at me. "He may be your baby, but he's not your gift. Babies grow out into the world, you see."

"And what's that supposed to mean?" I demanded.

"You people, you people," the old man shook his head. He looked tired and about as irritated as I was. I couldn't help feeling a little bad for him. I slid back into the booth as he continued to talk. "Here we are in this crazy, dangerous and unpleasant universe, and yet you people always manage to put yourselves square in the middle of it. Can't imagine why you do it." The man took a sip from his coffee mug. Tell me, Cutey-Pie," he asked, "do you pray?"

God, the man was nuts. I had no idea where this conversation was going. Why didn't he just order pancakes for his dead wife or start chewing on the plastic snowflakes taped to the wall? Why did he have to be such a talker?

"Sure," I said, which you know is true.

"What do you pray for?"

As if that was any of his business, but I just couldn't help myself. No one has ever asked me that before, not even you, and it felt good to tell. "Earl," I began "and Harold, and Keith, and Debbie who used to come in Wednesdays, but broke her hip last month. I pray for the kids at the daycare, especially the Pettits because their dad works out of state and their mom's got more than she can handle with the three of them and her dad is so sick. Then there's the Johnson boy who drinks too much and worries his mother half to death and the Clark girl who just can't manage to leave that good for nothing boyfriend who smacks her around. And of course, there's everything else outside of this town: war and stuff. I try not to think of it all too much, it wears me out."

"Me too, Cutey-Pie, me too. Do you ever get an answer?"

"Well, nobody's ever called me back, if that's what you mean."

"What if I were to tell you that you were the answer, or at least part of it?"

"What do you mean?" Crazy as this guy was, there was something about what he was saying that pulled me in. It was like watching one of those serial dramas on T.V. You know, where you just glance at the T.V. and find yourself glued to the couch for the next hour and turning to the same channel the following week to watch more. I just wanted to know where he was going to end up.

"We all have requests, Cutey-Pie. Some people spend their lives praying for world peace, some for healing. Heck, some even pray for that winning lotto ticket. More than some, actually. And praying's a good thing. Nothing wrong with a good, honest prayer, whatever the content, but most people miss the boat on the answer. They think that the answer has nothing to do with them." He took a another sip of his coffee. "Thing is, all of those problems you pray for, Earl, the Clark girl, the Pettit kids, you're part of the answer. We're all part of the answer. Nothing's getting fixed, healed, or cleaned up unless we're all included in the repair work, especially you."

"So what you're telling me is this baby is the answer to everyone's prayers. His being born is a miracle that's going to somehow fix everything up."

"Close" the geezer smiled at me over the rim of his mug, "but you're missing the point of the miracle."

"Go on then."

"I served in the army for a long time, Cutey-Pie. Don't ask where, I don't like to reminisce, if you know what I mean. Let's just say I was damn good at my job. I could show up when a fight was going down and turn the tide of things like I was flipping a coin. And most people thought that was a miracle. Truth is, Cutey-Pie, a real miracle isn't winning a battle you thought was lost. The miracles usually happened after I and everyone else cleared out, when they started planting things, let's say tomatoes, where the fighting used to be."

"So what does that have to do with a baby?" I demanded.

"Well, Cutey-Pie, this baby of yours, like any baby, is going to be a loud, messy disruption in the world."

"You can say that again." It was uncanny how the crazier this guy talked, the saner he sounded. It was almost as if we were having a normal conversation except for the fact that it made absolutely no sense. Until it did.

"Having a baby will make a mess of your life, right? There will be questions, gossip, and you can kiss your social life goodbye, Cutey-Pie. But that's what miracles do. They screw things up. If they're real miracles, they end with the mighty sitting in the dirt and the downtrodden dancing. They end with people planting tomatoes in the battle fields.

"Miracles make a mess. Things are different after a miracle, not the way they used to be. That's how it works. I can tell you that we all thought the darkness was fine and dandy until someone said 'let there be light.' Just saying."

"We?" I asked. I'd tell you I was making last ditch effort to figure out which family this geezer belonged to so I could finally get rid of him, but that would be lying.

"Don't worry about that Cutey-Pie, just answer me this, do you want to help? Do you want to be part of the miracle? Do you want to plant some tomatoes where tomatoes have no business growing?"

I wish I could tell you that I said yes just to placate him, that I didn't want to get him any more worked up than he already was. Truth is, I more than half believed him at this point. Whatever he was describing, it seemed so big and so wonderful, I wanted in. So you know what I said.

"Has the hen finished laying my eggs? demanded Earl from across the room. "I'm gonna start eating my napkin if she ain't."

That got me going. I remembered my job and finally went back to the kitchen to check on Keith and get Earl his eggs.

By the time I brought Earl his breakfast, refilled Harold's coffee mug, and finally returned to the stranger's booth, he was gone. His coffee mug was empty and he had left the 75 cents plus a generous tip. No one had seen him leave. Some would call that a miracle, but I knew better.

"That feller was just as sneaky as that goddamned deer head!" remarked Earl. "Did you know him, Harold?"

"Didn't he play taps at the Memorial Day service last spring?"

"Might could be."

And that should have been the end of it. A walky-talky who came in and left. It's happened before and will happen again, sure as anything. But, a couple days ago I took one of those tests and then I took it again just to be sure. And it doesn't make any sense with the pills and the fact that I'm not seeing anyone, but it came up the same both times. So I don't know how to say it, and truth be told you probably won't believe me, but the thing is, Mom, I'm pregnant.

The Jackass Gospel // Amanda Zentz-Alo

It has been an amazing journey. I never thought I would get to see something like this. Not the stable. I've seen lots of stables, but these people . . .

Let me start from the beginning. Joseph bought me from a friend of his a few months ago when he found out a couple of things. First, that there was going to be a census taken and he had to take his family to Bethlehem to be counted. Second, that his young promised wife, Mary, was pregnant. He knew he couldn't safely get them all to Bethlehem without some help, so that's where I come in. Yep, I'm a donkey, but I'm a good one, and a blessed one.

Anyway, you should have seen how people treated Joseph in town. They pointed and whispered and their faces were full of anger. It's the kind of look you see when you're about to be hit because you're too tired to pull the plow or you don't want to do what you're being asked to do. I was surprised to see this aimed at a human rather than another donkey, but there it was.

I wasn't sure what I was getting into at that point. But this man, Joseph, had kind hands and spoke softly and encouragingly. So, I followed him and watched as the people made their faces.

When we arrived at his home, there was Mary. She was clearly waiting to have a little one, but there were a few strange things. Although Joseph was kind to her and assisted her, he didn't call her wife or talk about "our" child. And Mary, she just had this peace around her that nothing could faze. Whenever she would start to get worried about the trip or Joseph's cold kindness, she would put her hand on that baby and that strange peace would wrap around her.

Anyway, a few days later we started our journey. A long one. Eventually, we made it to Bethlehem. Of course we were later than most, because of frequent bathroom breaks and all the space was taken up indoors. So Mary and Joseph stayed with me out here in the stable.

They had grown closer over the journey. Whether it was just the trials of making it through the trip, the forced quality time together, or the lack of glares from other humans.

Joseph was not only kind and considerate, but during the trip, he became proud. Along our journey, that same peace had settled over him. The couple would spend their night times sitting close to one another and that unborn child and praying to their God. It almost made me want to be one of them, to understand what it was they were feeling in that moment.

Well, soon after we got to Bethlehem, Mary gave birth to the baby. I watched it all from the side of the stable; Mary and Joseph both praying, even through her pain; and then the cry of the little one as he entered the world. Once all the commotion was over they found some cloths to wrap him up in and decided that my manger of hay would be the best to lay him in for now. I didn't mind so much because I saw something in that human baby.

That was where their peace had come from. Now, I'm just a donkey and I don't pretend to really understand all of this, but I do understand the faces of humans. And this child's, it was the face of a human that any animal would be happy to work with. There would be no fear of being hurt, and there would be enough food. There would be work to do, but never too much; this was the kind of Lord and Master you wanted to find in your life. That was the kind of Master you would be willing to serve with all that you had.

Over these last few weeks I could see that the humans saw that, as well. These shepherds came by and just sat and watched the little one. And they walked away with the peace that surrounded Mary and Joseph. What was really neat for me to see, was that they walked away with the look that Jesus (as he was named) had; that they would be good Masters, as well. I would have hated to have left the stable, but I would have been willing to go with them after they had seen the baby and been changed like that.

Time went on and then, just a day or two ago, some older men showed up. They had the smell of fear on them, but when they walked into the stable, and saw the baby, they found that same peace. They offered strange gifts and then began to talk with Joseph over in the corner.

The smell of fear began to come back, but Mary stood up and walked over to the men, holding baby Jesus. She stood by her husband and he put his arm around her, and you could see the fear melting off of them. Then they all prayed together, and the men left, going a different direction than they had come from.

Last night, Joseph woke up in the middle of the night and I heard him. He paced for a little while and I saw him pick up and hold the baby. After a few moments I heard the crunch of the hay as he laid him back down again, and then Joseph came over to check on me. Something is trying to threaten the peace of this family, but Joseph's God won't allow that. This peace, this gift, this amazing little boy is too precious. So, we're all getting up in the middle of the night and getting ready to travel together again.

I never thought I would see something like this, a couple so filled with peace and hope, even with the challenges and threats they have faced. It gives me hope for other people who meet this baby boy in their lives. Maybe there will be more kind people of peace in this world because of him. I guess I can only hope, and wonder.

Left Behind... In a Boat // Daniel Tisdel

Don't judge us. We earned that right. I mean, put yourselves in our shoes. Our business is fishing. It's our sole source of income, our livelihood. We barter for other things we need with fish. Good fish. If we need grain, we give fish. If we need cloth, we give fish. If we need building materials, we give fish. Others come to us, trading their goods for fish. It's all a pretty fair business, as long as two-thirds of your business doesn't walk off because a stranger asked them to!

Now, don't get me wrong, I'm sure this Jesus is a good young man, but we've seen a lot of prophets come and go. He must have been pretty convincing to pull the boys away so easily but I don't remember him saying anything but "Follow Me!" And then they just dropped everything they were doing, leaving me, Zebedee, to do all the work.

I thought it was kind of a joke...they would be right back, I reassured myself as I went through now three times as much net, repairing and organizing them as I went. Unsurprisingly, I came in much later than normal, finally eating dinner after it had long gone cold. I told their mother what had happened, and she reassured me that the boys would return late in the night or sometime in the morning before we went out on the lake.

Just before dawn I went out on the boat. James and John were nowhere to be seen. I waited as the sun rose and the fish became less and less active. Finally I wandered into the village. I knew of a few who were always looking for extra work as I often had to turn them down unless one of us had taken ill or we had a better than average catch. But this day was different, as I could not run the boats and pull the nets by myself. I hired two hands, and went back to the beach. Our catch was pretty miserable that day, but I told them to come back the next day...and for years that was the norm.

Oh, here and there the boys would return and bring us news of their travels. They would even stay a few days and pull nets with me like the old days, but it was clear even then that their hearts were not in it anymore. Truth be told, the arrangement worked out well for me anyway, as we had more room and more food in the household due to the absence of the boys.

For their part, however, they were happy, but were continuously going from town to town asking for food and shelter. It was a lot to ask them to sacrifice, but they seemed happy to do it. Even so, between the inconveniences that we suffered and the difficulties faced by my boys, we thought it was only right if the boys were rewarded in some way for all of it. They believed that this Jesus was the son of God and when we heard him speak, despite our original skepticism, we believed that there might have been something to it. Jesus had a certain air about him, something difficult to describe, that made us feel comforted and challenged at the same time. We were willing to believe that maybe he actually was the son of God.

So we thought it was only fitting that if Jesus was the son of God, and considering the sacrifices of James and John, our sons might sit at the right and left hand of Jesus when he came into his kingdom. Imagine how much prestige we would get if and when that happened. Then I could stand on the street corner and point to my sons and say to everyone that passed, "Everyone, look! There, next to Jesus are my two sons!" And until that day came we could glow in the promise that the day would eventually come.

Jesus didn't seem too receptive to that idea. But He also didn't dismiss it out of hand. He gave us a quizzical look and said that we didn't understand. Well, surely it didn't hurt to ask. We had to put in a good word for our sons, even if we didn't totally understand. I mean, what was there to understand? If Jesus was going to come into his kingdom, that meant he would rule over the people like the kings before him had, whether he was the son of God or not, right? There had to be wealth, honor and prestige to come with any association with him after that.

But now I am troubled, though I am not sure exactly why. The boys have returned home to visit during the week of Passover. There is talk among the people that Jesus may have been arrested, but my sons aren't saying much of anything, beyond talking between themselves in hushed tones. When I ask about

Jesus, they tell me not to say his name in public or to mention them in connection with him, but they never give me a reason why. Well, I am sure that this will pass soon, and they will continue travelling with Jesus soon, eventually taking some sort of powerful position in his kingdom. It's just a matter of time.

To Bleed // Laurel Kapros Rohrer

There's a place in the buried west
in a cave
with a house in it in the clay
the holes of hands,
you can place a hand in hand
I bleed, I bleed, I bleed
\- The Pixies

My handwriting is black and messy on the wall. The marker smell is sharp and dark in the stink of the little bathroom. "We can bleed for days but never die," I write in big block letters. It is wet and nasty in here, but the sound of the voices and music aren't as loud, although some jagged notes still sneak under the door.

They won't find me in here I hope, even though I broke the rules, even though I had no money to get in. I've got no money for anything: clubs, concerts or even food sometimes. Not after all the doctors, the sticking, the tests and them never telling me anything.

The blood just won't stop, nobody knows why. There is always the purge, the flush, the gush, from my messed up weak body. I'm outside the outside, where I've asked so many questions they don't even hear me anymore. I never get better. Each day it is worse.

I made it tonight, snuck past the big hairy guy at the door and slipped through the crowd to hide here, because she is going to be here tonight. As soon as I saw the flyers downtown, with her strange dark face, I knew I had to come. Knew maybe this would be my only chance.

I got here somehow. Small and invisible, I slipped in, sweatshirt pulled down to cover the scars on my arms. Always small, I fit into tight spaces. My clothes hang big, but inside I hide, hoping there's safety for my tired bones.

When I got into the club, it was too loud, too dark, too many people crashing around with skin slick up against me. So,

I scrambled into the bathroom and found myself in the dirty mirror. My young face was old and dry. I don't have the years that my face says I do, but you wouldn't know it if you could see me. I guess it's all trickled out of me, slip slid away with all that blood.

So now I hunch here in the stall, with my sharpie, my scrawl and my sliding away body, waiting for her to come and for her music to start. I heard about her long before I heard her music for the first time. Everyone on the streets was talking and saying her name, I'd seen it written on the walls of buildings.

"Her concerts will change your life," they said. "Her music will set you free," they cried. And the first time I heard it, it was a weird crazy spin of sound, up to the sky and back. The deep strum of a bass guitar, thump of drums and that voice over the top, that wasn't really a man or a woman.

She sang about rescue and forgiveness, but also about blood and hurt. Her voice, her song, made me feel that I might make it in the end, that it all might not slip away, like my own blood, my money, my lost family.

There is buzzing on the other side of the door to the bathroom, the crowd sounds shifty and restless. She was supposed to be here already, supposed to sing an hour ago. The opening band was weak and silly, or maybe they just seemed that way in comparison.

The crush of bodies murmurs and complains, drinks more and grows louder. Then suddenly, there is a change. There is shouting and bodies slam together even harder. It starts small, but soon voices scream to the rafters "She has come," and "she is here."

My body is suddenly ridged and tense. I can't breathe. I open the stall door a crack and stare at the closed bathroom door. But then, the scratched-up door pounds open and someone crashes through with a rush of hair and the smell of wood smoke and brown leather. I quickly slide the door lock shut and hunker down at the back of the stall, trying to quiet my loud breath.

"Too much, too many, they all want too much from me!" Her body slams the stall where I crouch and slides down to the wet concrete floor. The fringe from her jacket covers the floor by the toe of my sneaker and I know who it is. I lean to the side of stall, afraid to be too near. The crowd outside the door is loud and gathering closer.

I can't stop myself as I reach out a dirty finger to touch the soft, brown leather of her clothes. There is a stopping and a lifting up. I suck in air and start to gasp and cry, a feeling I knew once, long ago fills me up: life, blood, and a healthy, whole body. A long gone hopeful memory of something young and free flutters up from somewhere that once was dead.

But then the jacket is ripped from my hand as she jerks up from the bathroom floor and screams, "Who's there, who touched me?" She pounds on the stall door with small fists. "Hey who ripped me off? You stole from me man, you stole from me!"

I had, I ripped off something big and important from her, and I was full of it now; full of wholeness, scared of her angry voice and of looking at her face. Was I in more trouble now? Who would save me from being saved?

Scared and crying cool wet tears down my face, I quickly pulled my feet up and crouched on the edge of the toilet bowl, hoping somehow I could be gone again. The bathroom door was pushed open and more voices filled the room, more thudding feet under the edge of stall door. "There you are baby! What's wrong?" This new girl's voice was as harsh as the hard click of her heels across the floor.

"Someone touched me." The voice was calmer, but still there was heat and anger. "Someone took something from me!"

"Well, we all want to touch you baby!" Hers was a sharp little laugh.

It was the last thing I wanted to do, but somehow I had to. My body was stronger now after I shook out my fear, I opened the door and looked into her dark face. She stood there, beautiful, soft and hard in her worn leather and dirty jeans. The crowd of bodies behind her was a big wall of angry, in dark clothes and scribbles of ink and hair. The girl next to her, with the sharp heels and high voice, tried to snake an arm around her waist, but she pushed her off.

I had nowhere to go, but to open myself up. The confession slipped out: "It was me." My voice shaking a little, I continued: "I touched you. I felt you."

She looked into my eyes and really saw me. Moving away from the sharp girl and the shouting faces behind her, she took my hand in her own hot one: "It's okay, you're with me now."

Legion // Daniel Tisdel

I was born with a name, maybe even a good name, though whatever that name might have been has long since been forgotten, along with any memories of my family or my youth. I guess I can hardly be blamed for not knowing much about myself considering what has occurred since then. Due to my circumstances, for many years I was called by another name, but that name shall not be uttered here.

Upon further consideration, for the sake of accuracy in the retelling of my story, I will say that name only once. . . and not yet. For it is a name not associated with me anymore, and was never really my name to begin with. There is much power in a name. Far more than people seem to believe. I wake in the middle of the night every night in a cold sweat, panicked that those days might return. I admit that recounting those times or even saying that name, the name they called me, the name identified with this body. . . terrifies me to the core. I am terrified often.

Now I am different. Now I am known by another name. After I met the man and my life changed, the people did not trust me in that region. They had been afraid of me for years. They had avoided being in my presence at all costs. . . and then several of them lost their entire livelihood in the demise of the pigs. So, I left there for another anonymous town in an anonymous region as an anonymous worker of stone. But you don't really care who I am anyway, you only care about who I used to be, which is fine by me.

I was once called "Legion."

You tell me that many refer to me as a Geresene. I am not completely sure what that means. I was from the city of Gadara, which would make me a "Gadarene." You might want to make that edit in your notes there in your hand.

I remember little from my childhood, as I said, but I remember the first time I heard the voices. I was in the marketplace buying textiles of some sort. I was relatively young, not a boy any more but not quite a man. I had some money but I am not sure now where it came from. I remember being dressed fairly well, perhaps my family had given me money for my purchase, perhaps it was my own. . . at this point it doesn't matter much. Anyway, as I was about to collect my items and pay, I had a voice in my head tell me to shove the merchant's stall over. Internally I wondered why that idea had crept into my head and I tried to dismiss it, but the voice returned and this time it was more forceful.

Instead of handing over the money or taking the cloth, I threw the coin purse over my head and laughed a deep laugh that was not my own. I could hear coins bouncing in the square in a musical way, but that music was far in the distance. I am sure that people were scrambling for a few of the coins, but my focus was squarely on the merchant and his table. In my head, I was only an observer, a spectator, watching the events unfold as if I had no control over them at all.

My body shoved the stand hard over, knocking the merchant over in the process. I had always been strong, but that day my body seemed so much stronger than it had ever been. I stormed through the streets, creating chaos wherever I went. I kicked down the mud walls of people's homes, I tore the throats out of pack animals, I screamed horrifyingly at everyone I met. I did not do it, "they" did it and I was frightened and saddened that I was forced to witness all the madness first hand. I had a front row seat to the end of my former life.

They caught me and put me in chains. It took ten men to hold me down. "They" (the "they" inside me) killed two of them in the process. My body was chained to a post in the middle of a courtyard on the edge of town. In what was the first of what would become many escapes, I tore the iron bands off my wrists and stormed into the wild.

Yet, I had to eat, and my new companions joining me in the husk that had once been my body, seemingly ate as much as I did. So, I was forced to come into contact with humans far too often. I would have preferred to die, but I was not granted such a luxury. Eventually I ended up among the tombs. My body would be sustained with a wayward goat or a unlucky wild animal of some sort, or I would raid the town for an offering. Sometimes people would throw food out of a window and bar the door, hoping that bit of food would be enough to deter me and my guests. Sometimes it was enough.

The voices got more and more numerous in the early years. So numerous, that I not only wished to avoid seeing the havok my body was forced to cause, but I also avoided listening to the cacophony of voices talking, murmuring, screaming and whispering all around me in my head. It was always loud and always busy. . . but only for me. Clearly, no one else could hear the myriad of voices. I could not sleep, sometimes for days. I felt as if my body was being dragged along with me in it. Sometimes the part of me that remained slept (if you can call it that) with my eyes open, while my body continued to move under the command of my many hosts.

I believe many people have these voices in their heads. Some may only have one or two and they may even be friendly. Some may have no power over those they inhabit, other than to suggest different courses of action, like a teacher or counselor, as an option. In my case, there were many, maybe hundreds and most were not friendly. And they took complete control over every aspect of my being. Perhaps the worst of it was that the actions of my body were not my actions and the words from my mouth were not my words. I lived in this hellish middle existence until the day the man came.

As he approached, I felt something different in my guests, something I had not felt before. It was a mixture of genuine fear and surprising awe. They knew at a glance that this man had the power of life or death over them. No one had evoked this fear or awe before. They normally looked down on others as inferior, sub-par creatures, barely worthy of notice, but this man was different.

It felt as if they physically moved as far as they could from him, as if they were afraid of being burned if they came too close. For the first time in many years, the voices were nearly totally silent. It would have been a wonderful time to simply lie down and sleep for as long as possible but the attention of my visitors directed at the man held my attention, too. The man was magnetic. On the surface he seemed like anyone else but something about him was riveting, and it was difficult to say exactly what it was.

Even though my internal guests were deeply afraid of him, his magnetism drew even them. We ran to him, to curse him, some voices even wanted to injure him, though most were too afraid to even touch him. And then he spoke, and his power was made known. It was as if his words were made of pure light, burning bright light. I would have shaded my eyes if I had any power over my arms. I cowered internally with my visitors, wondering what was about to happen. I had never experienced anything like this in anyone else.

Almost at once, the man spoke and I felt myself emptying out like a pitcher. I was so shocked at the change that the next several minutes passed without my comprehension. I had to relearn, and quickly, how to stand, how to speak, how to breathe. I collapsed onto the ground and wept for some time.

When I regained my composure, I realized that I was covered in mud, blood and dirt. I didn't want to think about where the blood came from or whose it was. I washed quickly in a local spring and wrapped a piece of rough fabric around myself, as I was naked. Soon I would have to do something about my hair, which had grown down to my waist, but now was not the time.

I chuckled to myself at my newfound independence, but the townspeople still looked at me as the monster I once was. No matter what I said to them, they would never trust me. So I planned to leave, to find a place to live out my days. I tried to travel with the man, as now I craved the bright light of his words that I witnessed, but he asked me instead to tell my family and friends about what had happened to me. The funny thing was that I had no friends and did not remember who or where my family was. So instead, I told whoever I met all about the man and what had happened to me as I travelled around, trying to find a place to settle down and live a quiet life.

I thought I had gotten past that point, that no one knew anything about my past anymore, but my short time wandering and telling my story to anyone who would listen must have made a lasting impression. You followed your leads, found me and heard my story. Now I will get back to work.

Please don't tell others where you found me, I still relish this quiet anonymous life. But if you have any news about the man, please let me know. I'd like to see him again, even at a distance.

The Parable of Lazarus and the Rich Man //
Thom Longino

Then Jesus told them this parable: Once there was a teen named Lazarus. Lazarus was a queer trans youth who grew up in a small southern town. Lazarus was bullied in school, and was eventually kicked out of his home by his parents. With some meager savings he had left from a summer job and hope in his heart, Lazarus bought a one way bus ticket to San Francisco, the supposed Promised Land for queer folks. Once he got off the bus, there was no "Welcome to San Francisco" sign, as he might have imagined. After he found what he thought might be a safe place to sleep for the night, Lazarus fell asleep, only to wake to someone stealing his backpack. As weeks turned into months, and months turned into years, Lazarus learned to navigate his way around the city: learning where to get good oatmeal for breakfast, and from whom to get a blanket and socks on occasion.

To numb the pain of rejection, Lazarus turned to heroin, and to support his habit Lazarus would sometimes trade money for sex. Somewhere between shooting heroin and sex, Lazarus became HIV positive.

As time passed, Lazarus became weaker and weaker by being ravaged by street life and his battle with HIV. To escape the noise and temptations of the Tenderloin, he began sleeping on the outskirts of Pacific Heights. Occasionally, he was shooed off by the police, but he kept going back there because he discovered he could eat well out of the garbage cans, especially outside the home of Dives.

Dives came to tolerate Lazarus's sleeping outside his home, but would never acknowledge him when he either walked by or pulled out of his driveway in his Mercedes. Sometimes Lazarus' only solace was the family of rats he befriended, who lived in the bushes around the perimeter of Dives's house and they would sleep near Lazarus some nights to keep him warm.

The night before which Dives was to throw a big party, he passed away outside due to the cold air in his lungs. Because he was a good devoted church member, Dives was surprised when he found himself tormented, looking up into heaven to see Lazarus being consoled by Sara and Abraham.

Dives called out to Sara, "Mother Sara, please send Lazarus here to relieve my suffering."

Sarah replied, "No, for in your earthly life, you stored up treasures for yourself, while Lazarus lived through hell on earth, and he is finally finding love and comfort. Besides, there is a wide chasm between us that cannot be crossed."

Dives pleaded, "Then please, send Lazarus to my friends so they may learn from my torture and so they may change their lives."

Sara replied, "They have Jesus, Buddha and other teachers to help them."

Dives replied, "I know my friends are hard headed, but if they see someone coming back from the dead, they might believe!"

Sara said, "If they do not listen to the ways of compassion and unfolding love, they will not be convinced if someone comes back from the dead."

Acts and Letters

The Testimony of Bachos // Richard Cleaver

The following is a translation of a translation. The sole surviving version of this text is a Sahidic translation of what is presumed, on the basis of some unidiomatic expressions and the use of a few non-standard Coptic letterforms to render names, to be a Meroitic original. The original manuscript was found in a jar among the ruins of Anba Hadre monastery near Aswan. This MS. dates almost certainly from the late 12th or early 13th century; the underlying original is plainly much older. It seems likely the translator was a refugee from one of the Christian Nubian kingdoms that at that period were coming increasingly under pressure from their Muslim neighbors, although Alodia, the southernmost of these kingdoms, was not conquered until around 1500 and not completely Muslim until centuries later.

The anonymous translator undoubtedly believed it was important to preserve a text so vital to Christian history by rendering it into a less isolated language. There has been no attempt by the translator to "clean up" the occasional divergence from the account found in Acts 8 (notably the absence of the sudden and miraculous disappearance of Philip), to make the views of Bachos more "orthodox" by later standards, or to introduce passages from Christian scriptures that would not have been written down, or at least available in Meroe, at the early date of the text, which seems from internal evidence to date from around A. D. 85. Thus we apparently have in the *Testimony of Bachos* an invaluable independent account of an important incident in early church history, not to mention an expression of a pure and early version of the Christian *kerygma*.

I was present at the Final Testimony of the Great Bringer of Good Tidings, Bachos the Treasurer, before The Mistress of Kush, Lord of the Two Lands, Son of Ra, Amanikhatashan Kandake, and this is a true account thereof. I was among the crowd in the Royal Audience Chamber when the envoy from the Overseer of the Church of Alexandria came to rebuke us. We never understood why he demanded audience of the Kandake, as she has nothing to do with the Good Tidings in her kingdom, except, of course, that she welcomes all that is wholesome and conduces to the joy and serenity of the

Two Lands; for The Great Mistress of Kush is Queen Mother not only of the Royal Heir and his bride, but of us all. We do not share the Roman horror of female rule that was evident in every one of the envoy's words.

I was present, as I say, and here is what I saw. What I heard, you will have in his own words, taken verbatim by the Royal Stenographers as is usual at audiences.

The envoy's harangue was long—longer than any of us would dare to make to the Kandake, unless specifically asked, which he was not. But his ramblings allowed a grandnephew of the retired Treasurer to slip away in plenty of time to guide his esteemed grandfather to hear what the envoy was saying. It had been long since the retired Treasurer had left his room; he must now be past 80 and spends most of his time in prayer and receiving members of his flock. None had thought to summon him to the Presence of Awe until the envoy had made it clear that he was trying to refute the Great Bringer's own message, which is well known among us, even those of us who are not of his community. The crowd was so great that few noticed an old man, swathed in shawls and supported on either side by his grandnephew and the latter's wife, come into the Audience Chamber. Perhaps the Mistress did so, but she made no sign. Indeed, she did not make any movement or appear to acknowledge the slanderous and rude speech of the envoy, who called himself an Elder though he cannot have been more than 30 or 35 at the most. The Son of Ra is always gracious, even in the most trying circumstances. She could rarely have met one as trying as this.

When the envoy finished, he did not withdraw, but stood looking at the Kandake, apparently awaiting her answer. I was too far back to know whether his face—which should have been lowered, now he had finished speaking—revealed anything of his expectations of her reply. She, of course, said nothing. Just as someone began trying to take the envoy away, I heard murmurs behind me, followed by a rustle of clothing. Turning, I saw the assembled courtiers making way for a tall but elderly figure, not feeble but in no hurry. The Retired Treasurer was moving to the front of the Audience Chamber. His movement as he approached the dais was stately, and age had stolen nothing from his grace as he made the obeisance the envoy had neglected to make to the Lord of the Two Lands, Son of Ra. When she gestured for him to rise, the first movement from the Throne in at least two hours, the Retired Treasurer raised his high voice, still clear, resonant, and commanding so that it filled every corner of the Audience Chamber without any strain. These are his exact words.

Puissant Mistress, Kandake of Kush, Honored Mother of us all, I claim, by your benevolence, and in view of my former high position in the Two Lands, the right of rebuttal to the speech of this envoy from Alexandria; and emboldened by your nod, I begin, Gracious One.

My story is well known, but it may be that some of your younger servants have not heard it. After all, I have not come to court in some years. Your Puissance has been gracious enough to forgive the slight, in view of my age, and also generous enough to remind the court, more than once, of my many years of service to your Honored Ancestor. Even more, you have been generous enough to call that service faithful. That faithfulness I must now render to another Lord, not She of the Two Lands, but the Lord of all lands and all peoples, who in love gave himself even to a shameful death, never opening his mouth, that we all might be restored to the One who made us, and brought to live as sisters and brothers. I am not important, but my story is, especially when it can refute the slanders of this envoy. I am not important but I am left alive to bear witness, for love of the One God. Further, I make bold to remind all who hear me that the Good Tidings to which I bear witness, Great Kandake, were taught me by one who had them from the Savior's lips: the Noble Deacon Philip, who followed Jesus in his ministry and later was commissioned by His closest disciples to care for the Greeks in the congregation. This envoy has said he was set apart as an elder by one who was successor to Mark, who in turn was successor to Peter. This young elder-envoy is, therefore, but a disciple of a disciple of Peter. My teacher was a companion to Peter himself, and a disciple of the Lord himself. Have I not, then, a stronger claim to be believed? These Tidings Philip gave to me within the first twelvemonth of the Lord's rising. Are they not, then, more reliable than this envoy's third-hand tales?

This envoy from Roman Egypt is scandalized to find a woman in power. Of course the Mistress of Kush is also the Son of Ra, and thus both man and woman. I too am both man and woman, and at the same time neither. Perhaps this is why the

Lord of All granted me the favor of bringing me safely home to this hospitable Land of Kush to be a Bringer of Good Tidings.

How I came to be as I now am, some of you know, and the rest, those of you who are blessed to have been born in the Land of Kush, will be able to surmise. It seems this Greek, who comes from a Roman country, two societies where my kind are held in contempt, cannot imagine my situation here. It is not an important matter in itself, but for his education, and to place it in the record—for I see the Royal Stenographers are, as I hoped they would, taking down my words for the future—I remind him, or teach him since he seems ignorant of so much about us whom he presumes to instruct, that among us, a eunuch is by no means always a contemptible person. It is of course unseemly that a man should be close advisor to a Queen, unless he be brother or husband or both; and sending a neutered child to the Great Court is a gift many a powerful family, if they have sons enough already, makes gladly and without any loss of honor. So did my mother and grandmother with me. My honored mother had four healthy sons already, the eldest a promising cadet in the Great Queen's army (a promise he fulfilled for more than two-score years, only recently being gathered, weighted with honors, to the Bosom of Abraham). My grandmother too had offered her sons to the service of our country, and so they determined to dedicate me.

It surprises me that a man from Alexandria, the city where so many Kleopatras ruled as mighty queens, should be so ignorant as to dismiss Our Great Lady, the Son of Ra and Lord of Two Lands, the Mistress of Kush, as a genuine ruler and not some ceremonial Queen Mother. I may hope that being in this company today, and seeing how Your Puissance rules with dignity and is obeyed in love, will open his eyes. But I fear that something about how the Good News has been twisted in the telling by its wandering transmission by Romans has blinded his mind to the possibility. If so, however, how does he account for the Apostleship of the Women Who Discovered the Empty Tomb, being more steadfast than the male disciples who fled and hid?

But I go astray. As I was saying, the Great Kandake, your Glorious Grandmother Amantitere, was pleased to find me a person worthy of her trust and confidence. In the fullness of time, she made me her Grand Treasurer—not before I had proved myself suitable for the office by many journeys of trade and diplomacy on her behalf. From time out of mind—perhaps even our Roman guest knows this—it has been the custom among us to seal peace treaties, and maintain amity between us and our neighbors, by agreeing to an annual exchange of goods from ruler to ruler, in addition to private trade. Thus to work in the Treasury was also to be a traveler and to learn of the rules and the courtesies of diplomacy. That is the way of envoys between rulers—but of course, an Overseer of the Church is a servant, not a ruler, is it not so? This may explain sending an envoy who is ignorant of diplomacy, though not perhaps sending one who is equally ignorant of the humility proper to a servant of the servants of God.

Of course, I usually left such journeys to more junior servants of the Throne, once I became Treasurer. It so fell out, however, that a mission to the King of the Nabataeans took on a delicate nature, and after taking counsel, I appeared, not least because of my good knowledge of the tongue of that land and of the adjoining Roman province of Syria, to be the best person to go.

I had traveled to Petra of the Nabataeans more than once. Both there and in Alexandria—our envoy should know that I am not so ignorant of his country as he is of ours—and in many other places of trade, I had encountered the Followers of the One God, whom we call Children of Abraham, and I had learned something of their beliefs and their holy books. Fortunately, they have some of them in Greek, a language anyone in my position must know. Some volumes of this library I obtained, one here, two or three there, and studied over the years, gradually growing in my conviction that there was much truth in them. I resolved, then, that when my mission to Petra was done, I would go to their Holy City, sit at the feet of the best teachers, and offer sacrifice at the Great Temple. My beloved and gracious Mistress the Kandake was generous enough—generosity was second nature to her, may God give her rest and comfort—to allow me leave to carry out this plan, sending my report from Petra ahead of my own return by a confidential messenger who would accompany me. This messenger, it happens, now fills my place, being a nephew of mine, rich in years and loaded with honors by You, Gracious Son of Ra and Mistress of Kush. I see him standing at your left, and am happy to do him honor and praise his faithfulness and diligence in this early errand. The nature of the mission, and of the report he carried from me on his tongue—for we dared not commit it to writing—are not part of my story, however.

Three months I spent in Jerusalem. It is a beautiful city, and I delighted in the conversation of some wise elders, and happily acquired more volumes of their Holy Writings, most of them ones I had not known even existed. I cannot read their sacred tongue, but as I said, the books are also in Greek, for many of the Children of Abraham are now thoroughly Greek, having long been living in all the lands around the Middle Sea. These sacred books I read and reread, and asked my hosts to explain their meaning; and the more I spoke with my teachers, the readier I was to make my profession to the God of Abraham and take on the yoke of the Law.

One complaint I have of my hosts, however, and a grave one it is. I complain most of all of my teachers, for they knew what kind of person I am—my voice alone would be enough to make it known—and yet never did they give me a hint that might have warned me away from the deep humiliation that was to come. But then, they were not of the Temple party.

If you are to understand, I must say something about the Great Temple at Jerusalem. Those who are not of the Children of Abraham may enter the outer courts, and indeed many do. On them there is no restriction, save that they too may only use the special temple money when in the sacred precincts. Because the Law forbids portraying the human form, coins with the head of the Roman Imperator Caesar may not be used within the holy place. Special coins are minted, by leave of the Roman authorities, for use within the precincts. There are tables of money-changers in the outer courts, but there are also of course many in the city itself who will sell you the special coins.

The main entrance is at the south of the great platform Herod built about a hundred years ago, to make the mountaintop level and broad enough to accommodate the pilgrims and tourists who come either to pray or to stare. There is a terrace at that side, reached by broad stairs, and in the far wall are two gates, one of three arches at the left, another of two at the right. These lead into a closed area where more staircases lead upwards in three long flights to the outer court of the temple. Other passages lead from the lower vestibule to other parts of the three-story building that runs along this southern end of temple platform. This building contains offices, apartments for temple attendants to live in when on duty, and a pair of ritual baths. These are large tanks with steps leading down into the water that continually flows in, and then flows out again. One such bath is for women, one for men. Those of the Children of Abraham who intend to make sacrifice in the Temple, if they are defiled in some way, purify themselves in these baths. Those who are prepared to take the yoke of the Law also are bathed in them. It is in fact the principal part of the ceremony, so it was there I turned my steps, once I had entered the Triple Gate. Because in this Great Land of Kush, we practice circumcision already, it would not be required of me a second time, although I am told there is much debate on this matter among different schools of the Law, the followers of a teacher named Shammai requiring a drop of blood, those of another named Hillel regarding that as unnecessary rigor.

Now it was that I had that shock which, at the time, I thought was the end of all my hopes, although it was in fact the beginning of knowledge.

For proper purification, of course, one must descend into the bath unclothed, and go under the waters completely, including the head. Not even any jewelry or neck amulets or the like may be allowed to obstruct the cleansing waters. This is no different from our customs and I was not worried about it. The Children of Abraham, like us, are far more modest in general than the Greeks, who seem to find no shame in utter nakedness, but the reason for unrobing in this case is plain enough, and as the ritual bath is not visible to the whole world, there is nothing immodest about it.

Accordingly, I removed my clothes and placed them in the basket an attendant held out to receive them. As I turned toward the steps where the priests were standing, however, I was met with loud wailing and cries of dismay. At first, I could not associate them with myself, unless as a part of the ritual—perhaps a mark of farewell to my old self before greeting the new man? I kept moving toward the steps, maintaining as much dignity as I could without clothing and pretending not to be surprised by anything. If there is anything a diplomat learns, it is this.

I soon realized, however, that they were pointing at my legs and some were moving toward me to stand between me and the steps, making wild gestures to shoo me backwards and, in a few cases, signs that seemed suspiciously like those our people make against an evil omen. As the priests were speaking—shouting in fact—in the old sacred tongue, not the ordinary language of the country which I know, if not well, at least adequately, I had no idea what they were saying. They must have seen my perplexity because one switched to Greek and, in a low and quivering voice tense with urgency and, if I am not mistaken, horror, said, "You may not enter! Come no closer! The Law forbids it! You must leave at once! You are accursed!"

The word he used for the last was a rare one, and I took it to mean that I was ritually impure, so I answered, "Yes, that is why I am here, to enter the bath and be made clean."

"You cannot be made clean, no matter how much you bathe, you are an abomination!" he cried, even louder, as one does to a foreigner—as if shouting could make an unknown tongue suddenly intelligible. He turned and ran from the room, leaving me with the others, who went on scolding in a wild gabble. Such a confusion of gestures and voices I have rarely known, certainly in a holy place.

I simply stood there, waiting, as one does in a bazaar while rival vendors clamor for one's attention, until all but one subside. Was it my color that caused so much consternation? Perhaps. These Greeks and Syrians do not even bother to learn that we are more than one nation in our part of the world—we are all "Ethiops" to them.

Finally, an older, graver man made a gesture for silence, left the room momentarily, and returned presently with a partially unrolled book in his hand. He greeted me in Greek with at least a minimum of courtesy if no more, and said, "Allow me to explain. I am astonished nobody has told you of this before, but it seems a grave misunderstanding has arisen. The law states clearly, 'One whose private parts have been crushed or cut off shall not enter the Lord's assembly.'" He pointed to the passage in the scroll titled Deuteronomia—he was courteous enough at least to show me the Greek version—and continued, "You must leave; you cannot enter this place."

I could not move in my astonishment, so the clamor began to arise again. Somebody must have been inquiring about me in the meantime, perhaps the original Greek speaker, who had scurried back into the room while the older man was showing me the book of the law, because I heard people whispering frantically in Greek, loudly enough for me to hear clearly, "An important ambassador...minister to Queen Kandake...influential friends..." and similar intelligence. Apparently they were afraid of some kind of diplomatic incident if I were turned away, and yet the law was as clear as could be.

That forced me to collect my thoughts. I knew perfectly well that it was not absolutely necessary for me formally to take on the yoke of the Law to serve the Most High God. Many do not, especially among the Greeks who abhor circumcision, and who may wish to advance high in the Roman administration, where they will be required to make sacrifices to the Roman gods. For my part, if I undertake a task, I wish to do it thoroughly and correctly. That is how I gained the trust of Your Honored Grandmother, Mistress, and how much more suitable would it be in undertaking to serve the Most High God? So this bizarre law of theirs was grounds for disappointment. But I also understand that if our laws are to be respected by others who come among us, we must be prepared to do the same when abroad. I did not want to cause a scene, so I made some soothing speech that an hour later I frankly could not remember. Whatever it was, it seemed to calm them down.

My person, I felt, had been outraged. This prejudice seemed barbarous to me, as it would to many other people in the wide world whom I have encountered in my travels. And the rudeness of wording of their refusal was galling to my dignity. Although I was in Jerusalem on my own account, so to speak, yet I was an ambassador from The Mistress of the Two Lands, the

Son of Ra, the Kandake of Great Kush, and an envoy's person is sacred the world over. I determined I would not let my indignation show, however; it does nothing to maintain the dignity of an envoy to scold like a fishwife, especially in another country, as somebody should have told this envoy here from Alexandria, a city we are often told is the most civilized and cosmopolitan in the inhabited world. But a hint to the wise sufficeth, as the proverb says.

There was nothing for it but to put on my clothes with as much grace as I might, and return to my lodgings. For the next couple of days I avoided my hosts and teachers, making some excuse about an indisposition. I resolved to spend less time on the books of the Law—I had never read the one called Deuteronomia, as I had been told it was a later summary of laws found elsewhere—but to soothe my injured feelings with the books of the Prophets, who are poets and preachers of great power, both for rebuke and for consolation. The prophet Esaias I particularly found comforting, although there was much in his book that seemed disjointed and mysterious.

I saw no reason to linger in Jerusalem. Taking a final day to buy more books, and engaging a baggage cart and driver to help carry them, I retrieved the spacious traveling chariot I had bought in Petra, made of some light but sturdy local wood, flexible enough to made the ride easier. This wood was highly polished, with elegant touches of gilding here and there, and decorated with inlay work of wood in contrasting colors. I had fitted it out with a pair of comfortable facing seats for myself and any traveling companion I might encounter along the way, for of course among us desert-dwellers, the duty of hospitality extends to helping fellow travelers.

So I roused my charioteer from his caravanserai—he was no more drunk than is reasonable for a man with nothing to do but gossip over the wine-cups until new orders come—and, taking advice from friends of mine and colleagues of his, we chose the longer but more traveled road to the port of Gaza, and from thence the trading route inland to Petra. There are more oases this way, and, more important to me at least, cleaner and better quality lodging in the somewhat larger towns that route enjoys. I was leaving sooner than I planned; I might as well take advantage of the time gained to make the journey more comfortable, especially as I was still somewhat agitated by the incident at the Temple. I needed time to gather my thoughts before resuming my duties as ambassador to Nabataea.

The road down to the coast from Jerusalem, which is high in the hills, is sound and well-traveled, but not interesting. They call it a "desert road," but of course they have not seen a real one, like the road from this city to the port of Ptolemais on the Red Sea. That day the road was not even well traveled. I was reading the prophecies of Esaias, but becoming less and less clear about some of them, and my mind began to wander. Reading in a moving chariot, even over a good road, can be difficult. Maybe that was why the book was giving me a headache. At any rate, the text perplexed me. I caught myself reading the same passage over and over again, as one does when only half attending.

I asked the charioteer to stop for a moment so I could step down and refresh myself briefly. As I did so, I saw a man sitting by the side of the road, seeking some shade under a small shrub. He greeted me politely—I suppose my dress and the fineness of my chariot told him I was a person of some consequence—and asked what I had been reading. Apparently he had heard my voice as I came along the road. I have been told it carries.

He spoke to me in Greek, no doubt because I was reading aloud in that language. His was that of a native speaker, and he was clean-shaven like a Greek, and wore his brown curls cut short over his forehead in the Greek manner. I was not surprised to see one of the Children of Abraham looking so; many do, though there is some hostility between them and their cousins who wear beards and long hair. These seem to regard the Greek-speakers as not really Children of Abraham at all. There are many rival factions among this people at the moment, which is how the Romans managed to subdue them, but I will not bore you with the details.

I handed the man the scroll of Esaias, still open to the spot where I had paused in my reading, and recited the last bit—I had read it so many times I had it by heart:

> Because of his ill-treatment, he opens not his mouth.
>
> He was led as a sheep to slaughter, and as a lamb voiceless before the shearer, he opens not his mouth.
>
> In his lowliness his judgment was taken away; who shall tell his posterity?
>
> For his life is taken away from the earth; from the lawlessness of my people, he was led to death.

The man nodded as he followed along, and looked up at me. He must have seen some perplexity in my face, for he said, gently, "Do you understand what it means?"

I sighed and said, "Not really. I confess I am still a neophyte and in need of a teacher. Perhaps you can explain to me, since you seem to be one of the Children of Abraham, for all that you look like a Greek. Is the prophet speaking of himself, or somebody else?"

"Somebody else," came the instant answer. "One whom the prophet said would come. That prophecy has finally come to pass, but only lately. A man named Jesus son of Mary has recently been among us, and we know now that he was born to fulfill this prophecy and many others. He himself said so, when he first revealed himself in public, only four or five years ago. He came from a small town in Galilee, in the north, called Nazareth. When he was called to read in the synagogue one day, he asked for this same book you are reading, the book of Esaias, opened it, and read this." He unrolled the book to a passage some little way along from the one I had been reading, found the place he wanted, and read aloud,

> The spirit of the Lord is upon me; he has anointed me to preach glad tidings to the poor; He has sent me to heal the broken hearted, to proclaim liberty to captives, and recovery of sight to the blind;
>
> To call an acceptable year of the Lord, and a day of restoration; to comfort all them that mourn;

That there be given to the mourners of Zion glory instead of ashes, the anointing of joy to the mourners, a robe of glory instead of a spirit of despair;

And they shall be called generations of righteousness, a plant of the Lord for glory.

"Then Jesus rolled up the book, handed it back, and said to the people gathered in the synagogue, 'This prophecy is fulfilled in your hearing today.' They were so angry at what they considered his temerity that they drove him not only from the synagogue, but from the town, and would have thrown him off the cliff at the edge of it, one who was there later told me, but Jesus calmly walked through the crowd and left his hometown behind. So you see that the promised savior began to suffer even from the beginning of his preaching. But we say of him that he fulfilled also the words of this psalm"—you should know, Great Lady, that a "psalm" is what they call a poem from their collection of hymns—and the man chanted the following verses:

The stone that the builders rejected is become the cornerstone;

The Lord has done this and it is marvelous in our eyes.

"How do you know all this?" I asked. The man told me he came from the new city of Tiberias, near Jesus's hometown, and had joined the crowds following Jesus throughout the neighborhood and places farther afield. Eventually, after Jesus was treacherously handed over to the Romans, tortured, and executed in the most shameful way the Romans can administer, my new teacher had remained with some of his followers and eventually been appointed one of those who made sure the Greeks among them were not neglected. Later he went to a despised people called Samaritans and told Jesus's story among them—which was not new to them, for Jesus had preached there as well, scandalizing many of his followers.

Of course I wanted to hear more about this Jesus and how he fulfilled the prophecy I had been reading. I must tell you, Mistress of Kush, that although I did not fully understand it, the book of Esaias had stirred me deeply, in spite of its obscurity in parts. That indeed was why I was reading it again, to know it better in the hope of understanding it at last. But I was missing the key. This wayfarer encountered by the side of the road—not by chance, I now understand, but by the good gift of God—had the key I had been seeking. So I introduced myself, asked him if he were continuing in my way, and if so, whether he would do me the honor of accepting a ride in my chariot, so we could continue the conversation. The man, who told me his name was Philip, was glad to accept, and sat beside me as we traveled on.

Philip rolled the book back again, pointed out a passage, and asked me to read it with all he had said in mind. The passage went like this; it is long and I will recite only the high points:

> Hearken to me, O islands; attend, O nations: after a long time it shall come to pass, the Lord says: from my mother's womb he has called my name;

> He has made my mouth as a sharp sword, and he has hid me under the shadow of his hand; he has made me as a choice shaft, and he has hid me in his quiver;

> The Lord that delivered you, the God of Israel, says, Sanctify the one who is abhorred by the nations that serve princes: kings shall behold him, and princes shall arise, and shall worship him, for the Lord's sake: for the Holy One of Israel is faithful, and I have chosen you.

> The Lord says, In an acceptable time I heard you, and in a day of salvation I helped you,

> Saying to those in bondage, Go forth; and bidding those in darkness to show themselves. They shall be fed in all the roads, and in all the paths shall be their pasture.

> They shall not hunger, neither shall they thirst; the one that has mercy on them shall comfort them, and lead them by springs of water.

> And I will make every mountain a road, and every path a pasture to them.

> Behold, these shall come from far: from the north and the west, and others from the land of the Persians.

> Rejoice, you heavens; and let the earth be glad: let the mountains break forth in joy; for the Lord has had mercy on the people, and has comforted those of low degree.

Philip drew my attention to the phrase we had read in the other passage Jesus had chosen in the synagogue, "an acceptable time." This, he told me, referred to the fact that God always works just when the need is greatest, and had chosen to send Jesus with this message because the loving, hopeful promises of the prophets had grown dim in the hearts of the people, and rules and laws had taken their place—worse, arguments over which rules and laws were the most important. He read again the verse that spoke of being abhorred by the nations, and said this was another prophecy of how the people would treat Jesus, as indeed they had done, beginning with their driving him from his home. "That is why we say he is the stone that was rejected," he said.

I could not keep silent any longer. "I too know how it is to be rejected." And I told him what had happened to me in Jerusalem, and how it could not be, apparently, that I, who had no seed, could have any part in the covenant the prophet speaks of.

He said, "But do you not see how well the passage you were puzzling over when we met fits you? You too opened not your mouth, and turned away, you who had been dumb before your shearer; you too were denied justice in your humiliation, and were denied your posterity, just as the One the prophet sings of in his song. But that is not the end of the matter," he said, and rapidly scrolled forward until he found another passage:

> Let not the stranger, who would be joined to the Lord, say, Then will the Lord separate me from his people; and let not the eunuch say, I am a dry stem.
>
> The Lord says to all the eunuchs that keep my sabbaths, and choose what I desire, and hold fast to my covenant:
>
> I will give to them in my house and within my wall a notable place, better than sons and daughters: an everlasting name will I give to them, and it shall not fail.

Philip was speaking faster and faster now. He was too excited and absorbed to see that I was weeping openly at the promise the Lord made to me, me personally, through the mouth of Esaias. He was telling me now about the life and suffering and death of Jesus, how it had happened just as Esaias had said, how Jesus, like the lamb, and like me, had been denied justice, and been cut off from the people by the shameful death on a cross that, according to the Law in that same Deuteronomia, meant neither he nor his descendants were any longer part of the People of God but cursed. Like me, it had seemed that none would be able to tell of his posterity, for he would have none, seeing as he was not married, according to Philip. But then the stone rejected became the cornerstone, Philip said, and he told me how another prophet I had not yet learned of, Jonas by name, had spent three days in the belly of a sea-monster of some kind and that this had prefigured three days Jesus would spend in the tomb, as proved by the women who came to anoint the body and found the tomb empty.

Philip spoke too of the foolishness of the male followers of Jesus, who considered the women hysterical and refused to believe their testimony, being only women, "for," he said, "just as those priests despised you, a eunuch, so they and many another man believe women to be less than men, although the Lord spent much time, against custom, in their company—even the company of a Samaritan woman." This was the second time he had mentioned Samaritans; I confess, Great Mistress, that I did not understand at the time, but I later inquired and learned that these are another branch of the People of God, and the two branches will have nothing to do with one another, rather like this messenger from Alexandria threatens to have nothing to do with us, though we did not even ask him. Jesus, however, made the Samaritans the heroes of some of his teaching stories, and as Philip said, spent time with one of their women, teaching her so she would be able to spread his Good Tidings among her people. But I am getting away from my story. Forgive me.

The point I was about to make is this: you must know, Mistress of Kush, that in their country they do not accord women the equal place and honor that we do. Our Kandake is equal to any king, and a woman as much as any man may be the Son of Ra at God's good pleasure. Everybody knows this, except this Alexandrian apparently. Or perhaps he knows but wishes to force his prejudices on us. I can testify that Philip's teaching to me was utterly different—all people, eunuchs, women, foreigners, all are welcome to join themselves to the People of God if they wish to do so, and having done so, all are full and equal participants in the Body of Christ. This is only one of the customs that shows that new life in Christ is not the old way of rulers and ruled, powerful and powerless, or even the way of immemorial tradition and law. The Lord, Philip said, makes all things new.

"You see, then, that the Lord and you have much in common, and in fact we believe we all can share in his triumph, not only by understanding our own sufferings through his patient bearing of insult and torture, but in another, deeper way, by going down into the waters of baptism, dying, and being reborn from them, as he went into the tomb and then left it empty."

"You mean the water of the mikveh?" I asked, remembering the bath of purification that I had been about to enter before going up to the Temple, before I was turned away.

"That is an outward form of it, yes, but any water will do," he replied. "And there is another way we renew our encounter with the Lord." Philip then told me the tale of two of the followers of Jesus, the Lord's kinsman Cleopas and also the dear friend of Cleopas's heart, who on that same day were journeying to their home village, called Emmaus—I myself had passed the place, coming down from Jerusalem, he told me. Another traveler came to them and spoke with them of all that had happened, but until they broke bread together, they did not recognize him as the Risen Lord. Then they remembered that he had told them, just before he was betrayed to the Romans, to break bread in his name, and that it would become his body on earth, and more, it would make all who broke that bread together members alike of that sacred, risen, body. This all had happened less than a year earlier, according to Philip—a matter of months.

Finally Philip seemed to have come to an end, or perhaps he was simply worn out from his long speaking at such a pitch of excitement. However it was, he asked me then what I thought about all he had told me.

I inquired again, who it was of whom the prophet spoke; was it this same Jesus? For it seemed to me it was, and that if it had all come to pass as Esaias had said, the promise of the Lord to those who, like me, were called dry stems, must come to us also. As I thought of it, I began to weep again, for sheer joy. Philip put his arm across my back and held me as I wept.

Just about the time I recovered my composure, I saw an irrigation ditch along the side of the road, a little way ahead of us. I said to Philip, "Look, here is water! What is to prevent me from being baptized?"

Philip reached up—he was much shorter than I, who, like many of my kind, am unusually tall—put his arms around my neck, embraced me and kissed me on each cheek, and then, leaning back and looking at me seriously in the eye, asked, "Do you believe?"

"I believe that Jesus is Lord, the one whose coming was prophesied, who restores the outcast and the lost."

Philip signed the charioteer to stop, and both of us got down and went into the water. He immersed me in it, declaring that I was now united in baptism, through his death and resurrection, into the Risen Lord, and then embraced me again. We remounted the chariot and shortly after came to the fork of the road where our paths diverged. Philip asked to be put down and I dismounted with him.

"Before we part, Teacher, I have one more question to ask you. I see now that Jesus is the key to understanding the Law and the Prophets. But I live in a far-off country, as you know, and may not soon get further news of the Lord and his followers. If another claiming to speak for him should come, in distant years, how will I know what he teaches is true?"

"It will not be hard for you to discern. If the message brings joy and hope to the outcast, the despised, the powerless, and the neglected, it is the Good Tidings of the Lord. If it only satisfies the rich, the well-fed, the powerful, or those who think they are already perfect, it is false tidings and not of God," he replied.

Then, with a final embrace and a blessing, Philip turned right onto the road leading toward the coast, while I remounted, seated myself, and told my charioteer to go to the left, back toward Petra in Nabataea. Rerolling the book of Esaias, I began to read it again from the beginning, this time with newly opened eyes. I have never seen nor heard news of him since.

The rest you know, Son of Ra: how when I returned, I told my story to any who would listen—as how could I not, since my heart overflowed with joy, more upon each telling of it?—and in turn, baptized many into the Risen Lord. We have become a small but joyful and, I trust, useful band, sharing with each other what is needful, breaking bread as the two disciples did, and studying the writings that prophesy the coming of Jesus. Above all, because Jesus came to the outcasts, we have worked, not to give sight to the blind or hearing to the deaf or wholeness to the lame, since we are not miracle workers or healers like Jesus, but to make sure they are able to live among us with dignity, contributing their labor and their wisdom to the rest of us, as we all do. As everybody knows, many of us are eunuchs or widows or parentless children, and many slaves come to us. When we can, we buy the slaves their freedom—for the Lord came to break the chains of those in bondage. When we cannot, we treat them as if they were free. Among ourselves, we have no need of laws or rules, for love is our chief commandment, as the Lord taught, and as Philip taught me. If we keep that one law, no other is needed.

Now you have heard this person from Alexandria, purveying what somebody says another told him that yet another person had heard Jesus say; and he tells us that Jesus came to fulfill the law, not abolish it. This I also believe. But what does it mean? Are we to believe that God took on the life, sufferings, and death of us human creatures merely to clarify the rules of good behavior? Do we use a lion-trap to capture a mouse? If we did so, you all know that the mouse would escape through the gaps. It is evident that many laws and many rules cannot capture goodness and charity. Only love can do that. Neither punishment nor vengeance has ever made people better, or the world could long ago have dispensed with any laws. Fear breeds fear, repression breeds repression; as we sow, so shall we reap, the Lord has told us. Fortunately, in your peaceable lands, Great Mistress of Kush, Son of Ra, your benevolence has demonstrated the power of kindness over the rule of force and division.

Among the Romans in Alexandria, I hear, who extort ruinous taxes and fill the streets with armed soldiers, things are sadly different. This envoy from that great city may be the first who has come to us in many years—I do not know, since I no longer come to court—but we often go to Alexandria. There we have seen the quarrels and rioting in the public streets, carried out even by those who say, loudly, that they follow the Lord. If that is what he is bringing us as the true teaching, allow me to remind him, as well as all in my hearing, that Jesus told us that not everyone who called out "Lord, Lord!" was part of him, and that we should look at the fruits of their actions to know who is. Are brawls and demands the kind of fruit we look for among the followers of one who gave himself to all without counting the cost, even to a shameful death?

Great Mistress of Kush, Lord of the Two Lands, Son of Ra, you know my manner of life, and those with whom I live and work. You know how we have taken in those who cannot care for themselves, those who despair of life, those who are cut off from society. We are blessed to live in a society where such people are few, where hardly any orphaned children or widowed wives and husbands are left on their own by their relations. But such cases do occur, even in the best of worlds, such as we live in, and we have made it our business to join them to our family.

Because I was taught, and have taught in my turn, that true reliance on the Lord's saving work is only taught and learned by the way we live, you and all present who know me, know also that I hold no slaves, that I neither defraud nor degrade any person, male, female, or neither. You know that I welcome any person who comes to me to learn the Good Tidings, of whatever rank or background or state of life, and neither ask nor take any fee for my teaching. You know that I instruct them in what I was taught, and if they desire it with all their hearts, as I did, I baptize them into the Lord Jesus.

Further, my Lady, Lord of the Two Lands and Son of Ra, you know that many of those who came to me have indeed shared this regenerating bath, and we have become an assembly of believers recognized by all. We simple people who know the Lord and one another in the breaking of the bread are one family and one household, holding all in common so that none wants for anything we can share.

I testify also that those among us, and we are many, who cannot have offspring of our own discover that living this life and doing this work makes us whole. In this new family in the Risen Lord, we too can see and hear and caress the future of our houses. Another part of the prophecy of Esaias goes like this:

> Sing, O sterile one who bore no child; break forth into singing, and cry aloud, who were never in labor: for more are the children of the desolate than of the one who has a husband, says the Lord.
>
> Widen the space of your tent, and stretch forth the curtains of your dwellings: lengthen your tent-cords, and strengthen your stakes, and do not be stingy;
>
> For your seed shall inherit the nations, and you shall inhabit the empty cities.
>
> Forget the shame of your youth, and do not recall the reproach of your widowhood any more.

From being the servant of the Great Kandake, Your Honored Grandmother, Mistress of Kush, I have advanced to an even higher place: to be the servant of the lowest outcasts. By living among our people according to the pattern of the Lord whom I put on in baptism, I have found that I am no longer a dry stem, nor a barren reed, but the parent of many, and richer, if you will pardon my boldness in saying so, even than the Son of Ra. Know, too, that these people come to us not because they must, for they too, like any person, have their dignity and their pride, but because they know we will give them living bread and not a stone. We do not force them to believe with us, or to live by elaborate rules that come from some distant land, or follow customs that are not ours. We do not decree whom they may love or marry or acknowledge as their children or welcome into their families. We do not need to, for the once-desert cities of our hearts are no longer empty of sons and daughters, are no longer the habitation of jackals and kites. If they choose to share our baptism, it is because they see the joy that our lives give us, and the wealth of our poverty, and the love of the family that lives in our wide-spreading tents.

But this messenger from an alien city of Roman Egypt has not troubled to visit our tents nor speak to our people, so the witness of our lives is lost on him. He demands, instead, words rather than deeds, professions rather than fruit, a stone indeed rather than bread. So I will put what I rely on into words, in the hope that he may hear and be instructed.

Great Mistress of Kush, Son of Ra, this is the testimony given to me by the Lord Jesus through the mouth of Philip:

One: the Lord, by becoming a perfect human being, has lifted us up and restored us, all of us, the whole of creation, to God's perfect pattern, by loving us enough to suffer a humiliating death, then conquer it forever by rising from the tomb on the third day.

Two: this promise is open to all, not only to those some priesthood or assembly of the learned choose to find acceptable.

Three: by putting on our humiliations and accepting our injustices, he has brought out with himself from their tombs of oppression and want all the despised and outcast and downtrodden people of the earth, making them sharers in his glorious new life.

Four: all those who put on his death and rising in the Sacred Waters, and who share in the fellowship of breaking bread in his name, and live in the manner he showed us, become in him a new family, yes, even a posterity for those who once were called dry stems or fruitless branches.

If you graciously consider the rule of discernment Philip left with me, Mistress of Kush, you will see that my way of life and my teachings do indeed bring joy and hope to the outcast, the despised, the powerless, and the neglected. It is precisely they who have found a home and dignity and family in our midst. Whether the message of this envoy does the same, you, Son of Ra, will decide for yourself. But the people whom Philip taught me to consider the final judges are those of the same sort to whom the Lord came, who were the friends among whom he lived, from whom he chose his disciples.

This, Lady, is my testimony, given to me by the Lord's ambassador. I hold to it against the innovations of any Alexandrian Roman who knows nothing of our people nor our ways. It is for you, Puissant Mistress, Son of Ra, to decide which teaching you will permit in the Two Lands, but I trust in your wisdom and confide in your generosity.

That is all.

A Street Called Straight // Charles Featherstone

Ananaias pushed his way through the crowded streets of Damascus. In a hurry, he cursed silently to himself as he struggled to get around street merchants, crowds of shoppers, barkers and buskers and the occasional mad prophet calling down doom for the benefit of anyone who would listen.

These streets are always crowded, he said to himself. They were noisy and filled with the smells of animals, people, and food. And he needed to get to his destination before someone did something really stupid.

My destination, he thought. The house of Judas on the street called "Straight."

Some waved some cloth in his face. Ananaias brushed him off, intent on his destination. Not much farther now.

He knew Judas from their meetings. They were the tiny but growing community of people who followed "The Way," those who have come to believe that Jesus of Nazareth, who had been put to death by the Roman state only a few years ago, was the promised Messiah of Israel, the anointed one God would send to judge and redeem God's people, to judge the entire world.

But that same Jesus had not stayed dead for very long. His closest disciples found his tomb empty, and Jesus himself in their midst, speaking to them, walking with them, eating with them. The followers of Jesus, like this tiny community in Damascus, had long been convinced that in meeting Jesus, they had somehow met God Himself. They weren't sure what to make of it. They just knew it was true.

They would sometimes meet in Judas' house. And sometimes elsewhere. Their meetings were frequently secret, since they were increasingly unwelcome in the synagogues of Damascus, especially since the leadership of the Israelite community began violently cracking down on the followers of Jesus.

Some had even been killed.

And so, even as they tried living with the hope – the hope that Jesus taught them, the hope they repeated to themselves every time they gathered to break bread, drink wine, and remember their fallen and risen Lord, telling stories of his life, his teachings, his death, and his rising – their lives were soaked in fear. It's hard to live with hope when one is just nearly treading water, barely staying afloat, in a great tempest of fear.

As Ananaias wound his way through the noisy and crowded streets of Damascus, he thought of what awaited him at Judas' house. How to explain this? Especially to the others. Ananaias could hardly make sense of it himself, and he was operating on pure trust. What he'd been told that morning made no sense. Even how he'd been told. But how much trust would others have? Who would believe him? He wasn't sure he believed it himself.

He pushed through the crowds and finally, on Straight Street, Ananaias found the traffic thinned out. He didn't quite run, but he walked quickly. He was breathing heavily.

"I hope I'm not too late," he said as he entered the gate to the small courtyard in front of Judas' house. He pounded on the front door and waited. It opened a crack.

"Who is it?"

Ananaias didn't wait for a proper welcome. He pushed his way into the house.

"Is he here?" Ananaias asked?

"Is . . . what?" Judas asked.

"You heard me. Is he here?"

"Well, peace and blessings in the name of our Lord be with you too," Judas said with a little sarcasm in his voice. "Yes, he's here, in the back room. How did you know?"

Ananaias made his way past the guest room to the back.

"I'm not sure you'd believe me if I told you."

Judas followed him.

"Did you know he was coming? Who told you? How'd

you know he'd be here? And, why my place?"

Ananaias turned and looked at his friend.

"Why here? Maybe because you're still on good terms with the synagogue leadership, and so you couldn't been seen to turn him away. How do I know? Our Lord came to me in a vision this morning, and told me. You want to argue with this, take it up with Jesus. Now, show me where he is. "

Judas pointed down the hallway. It was a large house, and Judas had done very well for himself – his house had a small courtyard with a nice garden – as a tinsmith and merchant. His house was big enough so that the followers of Jesus could meet in relative safety, and Judas' position in the community of the Israelite diaspora in Damascus gave them a little bit of safety.

How long that would last was anyone's guess.

Ananaias found his way to the back of the house, Judas right behind him. He brushed aside the simple linen curtain in the doorway and beheld a man, in the robes of a Pharisee, his eyes completely clouded over, milky white, on his knees, praying.

So this is him. This is Saul of Tarsus. He just stood and looked for a moment.

Saul finished his prayer. He looked in the general direction of Ananaias, who found his the sight of his milky white eyes unnerving.

"Are you Ananaias?" he asked. His voice wavered a bit. He was afraid.

"I am," Ananaias replied. "And you are Saul. "

The man on his knees tried to smile.

"Guilty as charged. " He paused. "I've been told you will give me my sight back. "

Ananaias sighed.

"I've been told that too. "

Saul moved from his kneeling position to sitting, his back against the wall. He was clearly not used to being blind.

"How long do I have to wait for that?"

Ananaias turned to look at Judas, who shrugged. He then looked at Saul again.

"I don't know. We . . . we need to talk about this. This, your appearing here, we just need to make some sense out of all this. You understand that. We know why you're here, and you will forgive us if we're not sure we can trust you."

Saul nodded silently.

Ananaias let go of the cloth, and turned to Judas.

"The others are coming," Judas said. "I sent my servants to fetch them. They should be here shortly."

* * *

They sat around the table, each leaning on a cushion, bread and wine in front of them. Ananaias, Judas, Cleopas, and Andreas – all important people in the tiny community of "The Way" in Damascus. They sat silently, seriously. There was no joy in the breaking of bread. And a whole lot of fear.

Cleopas took a drink of wine. And then spoke first.

"No one knows he's here, right? Well, that settles it. We should kill him, right now, and dump his body outside the city after nightfall. No one will be able to blame us. And no one will miss him. Not at first."

Andreas looked at him.

"That's taking quite a risk. Even if we make it look like bandits did it. We'd have to take his things, some of his clothes. And burn them."

Ananaias shook his head.

"No one's killing anyone. At least not yet. . ."

Cleopas' face grew very intense. He took out a piece of paper.

"You see this? This is one of the warrants he has from the

religious leadership in Jerusalem, authorizing him to take the followers of Jesus – to take us – back with him! To torture us! Even kill us, like they did Stephen! Do you want that?"

He turned to Judas.

"Think of all you've created here! Think of all you've accomplished! They would take that away! Everything you've worked for, gone!"

He then looked at the others sitting with him.

"And if not for our own sakes, then think of our families – our wives and children, who also stand to lose everything! We cannot trust him. This man Saul is a murderer! We should kill him, while we have the chance. Before he kills us!"

Judas shook his head.

"If we do, there will be others."

Cleopas leaned back on his cushion.

"Then we'll deal with them too."

Ananaias looked at them. He set his wine chalice down.

"No. Murder is not our way."

Cleopas snorted.

"You trust him?"

"No, I don't trust him," he replied. "But I do trust Jesus. And he told me that Saul belongs to him now. I trust our risen Lord. Enough to take this risk."

Cleopas was not satisfied. Andreas and Judas sat fidgeting, uncertain and anxious looks on their faces.

"If it's any consolation, Jesus told me Saul would suffer much because of this."

"I'm glad our Lord spoke to you, but it would be nice to have some proof of what he said, Cleopas said. "I say we put this up for a vote..."

Ananaias shook his head.

"Cleopas, all we have of Jesus is the witness of those who

who saw him. And we trust that. And this is not open for a vote. I know this a risk, but I trust the one who calls us to follow. Something has happened here with Saul. I'm not sure what, but I trust. I know I am asking all of you to take a great risk. And not just for ourselves, but for our families. For all we have, all we have made, all we have built here. For everyone who breaks bread with us.

"But Jesus showed us another way when he went to the cross. He rose from the dead, and he tells us, over and over, 'Do not be afraid.' This is a time for us to not be afraid."

"We'll regret this," Cleopas said. "We'll regret not killing him when we had the chance."

"Maybe," Ananaias replied.

He stood up. The matter was closed, and he wanted to make sure everyone in the room knew.

"Now, someone get me a basin of water."

* * *

Ananaias sat and looked into Saul's blind eyes. Judas, Cleopas, and Andreas sat off to the side, there backs to the wall.

"You present us with quite a quandary, Brother Saul. We do not know what to do with you. If my brothers in faith here had their way, you would be a dead man."

Saul nodded. His body was shaking.

"I know. I am completely at your mercy." His sightless eyes scanned the room, and he seemed to choke on the words. "I don't deserve your mercy. Not after what I've done, and not given what I originally came here to do."

Ananaias looked at his comrades. This was the moment of truth.

"Today, however, is your lucky day. I trust you, in the name of the One Who Was, and Is, and Is to Come. I trust what Jesus told me about you, and I trust that he appeared to you on the road and called you to follow him."

Ananaias placed his hands on Saul's head. Saul closed his eyes. The other men looked on intently, a mix of wonder and disapproval on their faces.

"So, Brother Saul, the Lord Jesus who appeared to you on the road by which you came has sent me so that you may regain your sight and be filled with the Holy Spirit."

"Amen," Saul said.

He opened his eyes. They were clear, and brown, and they sparkled in the afternoon sunlight. He smiled.

"I can see! I was blind, and now I see!"

He looked at Ananaias and beheld his benefactor's face for the very first time.

"We're not done, Brother Saul. Lean forward." Ananaias scooped up some water. "And now, I baptize you in the name of the Father . . . and the Son . . . and the Holy Spirit."

With each invocation, Ananaias poured the water in his hands on Saul's head. Cleopas gasped.

"And now, Brother Saul, you are one with us in faith. With us, you now share in the life, death, and resurrection of our Lord Jesus."

Ananaias turned to Judas.

"I think our brother here needs something to eat. It's been a long day and he is going to need some strength for the long and hard journey ahead of him."

Saul leaned back, water still dripping on his clothes and running down his face. He smiled.

Ananaias took a breath.

"I still don't know what to make of you, Brother Saul. But I don't envy you. Jesus told me you would suffer much for his sake. Are you ready for that? Do you have any idea what it means? Because I don't."

Saul sighed and closed his eyes.

"We'll see what it all brings. There's probably no way to prepare for such a calling. But I know something – I'm his now, aren't I? I belong to Jesus, don't I?"

Ananaias nodded.

"Yes, you belong to him now."

Saul opened his eyes and looked at Ananaias. It seemed, for a moment, that as he looked into Saul's deep, dark eyes, Ananaias could see all the way to bottom of Saul's soul.

"Then that's all that matters," Saul replied.

3 Corinthians // Megan Rohrer

Dear people of Corinth,

Grace, peace and all that stuff I usually write at the beginning of my letters. I trust this letter finds you well.

Thank you for being so cool about all that unsolicited advice I sent you awhile back. I was going through a grumpy phase, because I was experiencing a lot of pain from a leg injury.

I am maturing in faith and have come to the conclusion that God is God, and I am not. By this, I mean to say that my near-God-experience, gave me a bit of a God complex. Some of my previous letters were written in my false belief that I was better than you.

I have since learned that we all make mistakes in life, love and faith.

Since we last communicated, I discovered that married life is much harder than I imagined. And, despite my best efforts we divorced and are now seeking to repair our hearts and put our lives back together. In the midst of my transition, it has occurred to me that I have begun to live into some of the traits I previously judged you for.

I am sorry.

Love is a lot harder than I thought. I have stumbled and mis-stepped, even when I was acting with the best of intentions. In my struggles, I learned more about God's patience, redemptive power and forgiveness than I had ever known before.

Instead of listing a laundry list of faults I found in your community, I wish I would have listened more to your pains and the lessons you learned as you reconciled with God and your neighbors.

I hope to visit you soon and share my apologies in person. Until then, feel free to share all my letters with others as a reminder of my arrogance and as a lesson to judge others less.

Thanks again for putting up with my youthful obnoxiousness.

Love in Christ and doing my best,

Paul

Revelations

Dreams of Dreams of Dreams // Megan Rohrer

What would happen if Martin Luther King, Jr's dream was taken as seriously as my dream in the Book of Revelations?

I told them over and over that it was a dream, but those who were certain God agreed with them, took my words and used them to yell at people who lived, loved and worshipped differently.

So, I will try again to tell you the story. But no matter how certain you become that God is on your side, please don't use my dream of a dream to convince others that God is against them.

On night I dreamt that I was responding to a devastating tragedy. Perhaps it was the aftermath of a terrorist attack, a terrible car crash or a tornado that stirred up a mighty chaotic wind. Whether it was spirit led, the result of a neglectful government or a malicious attack by those who fear equality, what seemed important in the dream was the act of saving.

As I ran past a child, I swooped them up into my hands and ran into a nearby recreational vehicle (RV). Inside, the child wept out of fear and confusion. I cleaned its scrapes and washed off the mud that coated their clothes. A few minutes later the woman I loved entered with another child and yelled over the chaos that it was time to go home.

She revved the engine and floored it. I grabbed the kids by their collars so they wouldn't roll to the back of the vehicle, as a flash of light enveloped the windshield so brightly that I had to turn away.

We landed in another time, near a quaint house. Surrounded by large shady trees and a bubbling river, the house seemed the opposite of the terror and trauma we escaped. Was this heaven or the future?

My head was groggy, pulsing and warning of an impending headache. "Here, take these rehydration capsules," said my beloved.

"What just happened?" I asked her.

"Thank goodness this was our last trip," she said. "I don't think you could take another leap."

I shrugged in confusion and she continued to explain. "We go back to the past to save the children that ancient newspapers tell us passed away in accidents and tragedies. We can't have kids of our own, no one can. And we decided that rescuing children in accidents who wouldn't be missed was the only ethical solution."

Somewhere in my achy bones, I had heard this story before. Then I remembered when the President announced in her State of the Union that NASA had unlocked the mysteries of Quantum Physics. Not only could they embark on journeys through space, but they had also been traveling through time.

Congress had been gridlocked for almost a century and refused to pass bills that to prevent the biggest disaster the world would ever know. They believed that if they did nothing, they could blame the other side of the aisle for the fall out.

Then, despite thousands of attempts to go back in time to fix it, the disasters kept coming and seemed to get worse. Civilians began travelling back in time, like I've read people used to travel on airplane flights. Four Horses Flights offered tours of time and space, while Trumpet Travels kept the records and conducted studies to assure people that the leaping was safe. We believed they were promoting a healthier future for everyone.

Those who were skeptical were won over by endless advertising campaigns.

Somewhere along the way, most of the population became infertile. Few seemed to notice, because when had been using doctors to make designer babies for decades. It took a few more decades to discover that the designer babies were incapable of reproducing without the support of doctors and miraculous medications.

While some people mourned the loss of "natural" fertility, others celebrated the evolution as an equalizer that ended the homophobia that blinded our ancestors to the ways they were thwarting God's creative order.

I snapped out of my flashback when I noticed the two children were gripping my hands so tightly that my fingers had turned purple. I sat them on the couch and introduced myself.

"We have brought you to a new time and space where you will be safe. We will be your mothers and inside the house, you will find ten brothers and sisters. The twelve of you will grow up to lead this world. When you grow and have your own families, you will become twelve nations and become the embodied love of God.

"It's ok to be scared. It's ok to have questions. It's ok to become the beautiful children of God that you were meant to be. Here in this land of milk and honey, God will watch over you and help you experience true peace."

The two children slowly peered out of the RV, seemingly looking for the danger of the days they knew too well. Their bodies relaxed when they saw that the pain, smog and devastation of the world they had known was gone.

They smiled as they skipped to the house.

About the Authors

Richard Cleaver is the author of *Know My Name: A Gay Liberation Theology* (Westminster John Knox, 1995), among other works. He began his life-long association with the Catholic Worker movement in 1975. Later worked for the American Friend Service Committee in Michigan for over a decade. Raised in Iowa and a graduate of Grinnell College there, he has lived all over the United States and also, on three separate occasions, in Japan. He holds the M.A. in Advanced Japanese Studies from Sheffield University in England. In 2003 he was ordained to the priesthood for the Orthodox-Catholic Church of America, a welcoming and inclusive jurisdiction in the Orthodox tradition that does not restrict ordination by gender, sexual orientation, or marital status. He currently works and lives in the U.S. Territory of the Virgin Islands. .

Malcolm Himschoot is an ordained minister in the United Church of Christ, with experience in local church, community, and denominational settings. His writing on religion and social reform has appeared in Prism, The Progressive Christian, Belt, and in the previous Wilgefortis book "Letters for My Brothers: Transitional Wisdom in Retrospect." He currently helps raise a family in Cleveland, Ohio.

Thom Longino is an expatriate of the Southeastern U.S. currently residing in San Francisco. Thom is ordained in the United Church of Christ, currently working G-d's graveyard shift as part of the San Francisco Night Ministry. He also serves as adjunct pastor of Ebenezer/herchurch Lutheran in San Francisco.

Kathryn Muyskens is a perpetual student of life. She is originally from Denver, Colorado. Recently she has been studying in London, getting her MA in Philosophy from the University College London. Writing is her passion and you can find more of her work on Elephant Journal, an online journal dedicated to living mindfully.

Emily Olsen is a New Jersey native currently completing a Masters in Biblical Languages at the Graduate Theological Union in Berkley, CA. She is also a candidate for ordained ministry in the

ELCA. Emily enjoys reading, writing, and pretending to be a dinosaur in her spare time. She is always up for an adventure be it Jurassic or otherwise.

Laurel Kapros Rohrer has an M.F.A. In creative writing from New York University. By day she is a legal secretary and in her spare time she writes, volunteers and does martial arts. She happily lives in San Francisco with her wonderful spouse and two furry cats.

Megan Rohrer is the first openly transgender pastor ordained in the Lutheran church, was named a 2014 honorable mention as an Unsung Hero of Compassion by His Holiness the Dalai Lama, received an Honorary Doctorate from Palo Alto University and was a finalist for a Lambda Literary Award in transgender nonfiction. Megan is the co-editor of Letters for My Brothers: Tranistional Wisdom in Retrospect and Holy Night: Prayers and Meditations for People of the Night and the author of Queerly Lutheran and With a Day Like Yours, Couldn't You Use a Little Grace.

Daniel Tisdel taught high school Spanish for fourteen years and then finally decided to change careers to something he had been putting off for over twenty years, ordained ministry as a Lutheran pastor. Other jobs he has held have been as varied as anyone; Electrician, Golf Course Construction Worker, Pizza Chef, School Bus Driver, Professional Actor, and Grocery Store Clerk, among others, but while "Writer" was something he often aspired to, it was something he never expected to attain. And there are a lot of stories (and even full books) still bouncing around in his brain, waiting to be released on an unsuspecting public... He grew up in Colorado, lived extensively in North Carolina, Florida and California, and has now gone full circle to live in the mountains of Colorado where he pastors a small church. He loves hiking and camping, woodworking, and playing and watching sports, but most of all he loves people.

Amanda Zentz is the pastor at Central Lutheran Church in Portland, Oregon. With a passion for baptism and funerals and a love for liturgy, Pr. Amanda digs deep into the traditions of the church to teach the deeper meanings of our ritualized actions. Growing up outside of the church, Amanda was baptized on December 14, 1997 while studying for her undergraduate degree in Theatre Arts from Susquehanna University in Selinsgrove, PA. Amanda went on to receive her MDiv from Pacific Lutheran Theological Seminary in Berekeley, CA in 2004.

WELCOME
A Communal Response To Poverty

Mission

Welcome seeks to provide a faithful response to poverty and to improve the quality of life for individuals in our community by providing: hospitality; education; food; and referrals for housing, health care and drug and alcohol treatment.

The Heart of our Work

Welcome teaches individuals and faith communities to respond to local poverty by listening to the needs of the community, creatively responding and whenever possible enabling those living in poverty to participate as equals. Welcome's projects utilize interfaith volunteers, are designed to somatically heal post-traumatic stress disorder and to be replicated.

Programs

Welcome's programs change regularly to respond to current poverty issues. While, many of our projects are based out of San Francisco, why try to travel to other cities across the country to share what we've learned and to help others replicate our projects. In order to increase our impact, we partner with often partner with other organizations.

The Homeless Vision Project: A nationwide project which has given away over 823 free eye exams and prescription glasses to homeless and low income individuals since October 2013. *A partnership with SF CARES and Project Homeless Connect.*

Transgender Education Project: A website to provide educational information for service providers and low income individuals in San Francisco who are in need of transgender related care. *A partnership with the San Francisco Department of Public Health.*

Just Lutheran: A multimedia online DIY (do it yourself) guide to enable congregations and individuals to respond to poverty. http://justlutheran.blogspot.com

SF CARES: A collaboration of St. Paulus Lutheran Church, Night Ministry, the Faithful Fools Street Ministry and Welcome, faithful organizations who are working together in order to increase our ability to help the underserved in San Francisco. We are particularly passionate about providing opportunities, resources and support for individuals who are poor, homeless, formerly homeless and experiencing mental health or brain disorder issues.

Urban Pilgrimage: Provides educational opportunities, seminary classes on diversity and urban ministry, certificates for trainings in urban ministry, curriculum for youth groups, pilgrimage opportunities, mentoring for groups and individuals and teleconferences. *A partnership with SF CARES.*

Hospitality Hour: Every Sunday morning, 90-140 individuals are served a two course meal at St. Francis Lutheran Church. A Community Thanksgiving Meal feeds an additional 200 individuals each year. *A partnership with St. Francis Lutheran Church and Food Runners.*

The Senior Program: Every Wednesday, activities, lunch and hospitality for seniors are provided at St. Francis Lutheran Church. *A partnership with St. Francis Lutheran Church.*

The HIV+ Grocery Project: Every Saturday we provide groceries to housed HIV+ individuals. Currently 56% of HIV+ individuals in San Francisco do not have enough food to take their medications on a regular basis. We hope to reduce this number. *A partnership with St. Francis Lutheran Church and Food Runners.*

The Welcome Pantry: Welcome gives away over 108,000 pounds of food each year to about 200 families living in the Castro the neighborhood. *A partnership with St. Francis Lutheran Church and the San Francisco/Marin Food Bank.*

Previous Projects

The LGBTQ Youth Leadership Project: A nationwide storytelling project since 2008, that collects multimedia oral histories with LGBTQ homeless youth across the country, encourages faith communities to create or connect with local shelters and creates curriculum for replicating the project.

The Welcome Center: Every Tuesday since 1996, guests are served a light lunch, get their mail, clean socks and blankets. Volunteers get to know guests and chat with them at Old First Presbyterian Church. A chaplain helps participants one-on-one, improve the quality of their life. This project is in partnership with Old First Presbyterian Church, SF CARES and the Faithful Fools Street Ministry.

Saturday Community Dinners: Every second and fourth Saturday since 1996, between 150 and 300 guest are served dinner. Congregations and other groups provide the food, volunteers and eat with our guests. This project is in partnership with Old First Presbyterian Church, SF CARES and the Faithful Fools Street Ministry.

The Church Security Program: Consultations with congregations about how they can make their congregation safe, agree on safe boundaries for pastoral care, respond to the effects of mental illness and addiction issue and provide mission based alternatives to night time security.

The Free Farm: A community farm created on the ashes where St. Paulus Lutheran Church used to be before it burned down in the early 90's. Since its creation in 2010, more than 6,093 pounds of free food have been harvested and given away to its neighbors. This project is in partnership with St. Paulus Lutheran Church, SF CARES, the Free Farm Stand and Produce to the People.

Vanguard Revisited: Vanguard Revisited was a project in partnership with the GLBT Historical Society, that enabled homeless queer youth to creatively interact with a group the history of the street hustlers who lived in San Francisco's Tenderloin District in the late 60's. This project will created a magazine, exhibit and nationwide speaking tour to highlight the poverty and issues that affect queer street youth.

Otro Vanguard: A weekly gathering of LGBTQ Homeless youth in San Francisco since 2010, that used art, poetry, video and engagement with the history to empower LGBTQ homeless youth to improve their quality of life, speak out publicly and become leaders.

Somatic Trauma Care: This one-on-one support for homeless and formerly homeless individuals enables them to gain the skills they need to heal from the trauma that causes and comes from life living on the streets. Designed to help individuals live fuller more independent life, participants in our trauma care often find they are then able to utilize other services and opportunities to improve their health, education and ability to participate in community.

You can support Welcome by donating online or by sending a check to:

Welcome
3201 Ulloa St
San Francisco CA 94116